Machine Learning Fundamentals

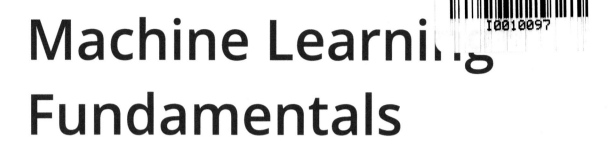

Use Python and scikit-learn to get up and running with the hottest developments in machine learning

Hyatt Saleh

Packt

I0010097

Machine Learning Fundamentals

Copyright © 2018 Packt Publishing

All rights reserved. No part of this book may be reproduced, stored in a retrieval system, or transmitted in any form or by any means, without the prior written permission of the publisher, except in the case of brief quotations embedded in critical articles or reviews.

Every effort has been made in the preparation of this book to ensure the accuracy of the information presented. However, the information contained in this book is sold without warranty, either express or implied. Neither the author, nor Packt Publishing, and its dealers and distributors will be held liable for any damages caused or alleged to be caused directly or indirectly by this book.

Packt Publishing has endeavored to provide trademark information about all of the companies and products mentioned in this book by the appropriate use of capitals. However, Packt Publishing cannot guarantee the accuracy of this information.

Author: Hyatt Saleh

Managing Editor: Neha Nair

Acquisitions Editor: Aditya Date

Production Editor: Samita Warang

Editorial Board: David Barnes, Ewan Buckingham, Simon Cox, Manasa Kumar, Alex Mazonowicz, Douglas Paterson, Dominic Pereira, Shiny Poojary, Saman Siddiqui, Erol Staveley, Ankita Thakur, and Mohita Vyas

First Published: November 2018

Production Reference: 1291118

ISBN: 978-1-78980-355-6

Table of Contents

Unsupervised Learning: Real-Life Applications 39

Preface

About

This section briefly introduces the author, the coverage of this book, the technical skills you'll need to get started, and the hardware and software required to complete all of the included activities and exercises.

About the Book

As machine learning algorithms become popular, new tools that optimize these algorithms are also being developed. *Machine Learning Fundamentals* explains the scikit-learn API, which is a package created to facilitate the process of building machine learning applications. You will learn how to explain the differences between supervised and unsupervised models, and how to apply some popular algorithms to real-life datasets.

You'll begin by learning how to use the syntax of scikit-learn. You'll study the differences between supervised and unsupervised models, as well as the importance of choosing the appropriate algorithm for each dataset. You'll apply an unsupervised clustering algorithm to real-world datasets to discover patterns and profiles, and explore the process to solve an unsupervised machine learning problem. Then, the focus of the book shifts to supervised learning algorithms. You'll learn how to implement different supervised algorithms and develop neural network structures using the scikit-learn package. You'll also learn how to perform coherent result analysis to improve the performance of the algorithm by tuning hyperparameters. By the end of this book, you will have the skills and confidence to start programming machine learning algorithms.

About the Author

After graduating from college as a business administrator, **Hyatt Saleh** discovered the importance of data analysis to understand and solve real-life problems. Since then, as a self-taught person, she has not only worked as a freelancer for many companies around the world in the field of machine learning, but has also founded an artificial intelligence company that aims to optimize everyday processes.

Objectives

- Understand the importance of data representation
- Gain insights into the differences between supervised and unsupervised models
- Explore data using the Matplotlib library
- Study popular algorithms, such as K-means, Mean-Shift, and DBSCAN
- Measure model performance through different metrics
- Study popular algorithms, such as Naïve Bayes, Decision Tree, and SVM
- Perform error analysis to improve the performance of the model
- Learn to build a comprehensive machine learning program

Audience

Machine Learning Fundamentals is designed for developers who are new to the field of machine learning and want to learn how to use the scikit-learn library to develop machine learning algorithms. You must have some knowledge and experience with Python programming, but you do not need any prior knowledge of scikit-learn or machine learning algorithms.

Approach

Machine Learning Fundamentals takes a hands-on approach to introduce beginners to the world of machine learning. It contains multiple activities that use real-life business scenarios for you to practice and apply your new skills in a highly relevant context.

Minimum Hardware Requirements

For the optimal student experience, we recommend the following hardware configuration:

- Processor: Intel Core i5 or equivalent
- Memory: 4 GB RAM or higher

Software Requirements

You'll also need the following software installed in advance:

- Sublime Text (latest version), Atom IDE (latest version), or other similar text editor applications
- Python 3
- The following Python libraries: NumPy, SciPy, scikit-learn, Matplotlib, Pandas, pickle, jupyter, and seaborn

Installation and Setup

Before you start this book, you'll need to install Python 3.6, pip, scikit-learn, and the other libraries used in this book. You will find the steps to install these here:

Installing Python

Install Python 3.6 by following the instructions at this link: https://realpython.com/installing-python/.

Installing pip

1. To install pip, go to the following link and download the **get-pip.py** file: https://pip.pypa.io/en/stable/installing/.
2. Then, use the following command to install it:

```
python get-pip.py
```

You might need to use the **python3 get-pip.py** command, due to previous versions of Python on your computer are already using use the **python** command.

Installing libraries

Using the **pip** command, install the following libraries:

```
python -m pip install --user numpy scipy matplotlib jupyter pandas seaborn
```

Installing scikit-learn

Install scikit-learn using the following command:

```
pip install -U scikit-learn
```

Installing the Code Bundle

Copy the code bundle for the class to the **C:/Code** folder.

Additional Resources

The code bundle for this book is also hosted on GitHub at: https://github.com/TrainingByPackt/Machine-Learning-Fundamentals.

We also have other code bundles from our rich catalog of books and videos available at https://github.com/PacktPublishing/. Check them out!

Conventions

Code words in text, database table names, folder names, filenames, file extensions, pathnames, dummy URLs, user input, and Twitter handles are shown as follows: "Import the **iris** toy dataset using scikit-learn's datasets package and store it in a variable named **iris_data**."

A block of code is set as follows:

```
from sklearn.datasets import load_iris

iris_data = load_iris()
```

New terms and important words are shown in bold. Words that you see on the screen, for example, in menus or dialog boxes, appear in the text like this: "Below the dataset's title, find the download section and click on **Data Folder**."

1

Introduction to Scikit-Learn

Learning Objectives

By the end of this chapter, you will be able to:

- Describe scikit-learn and its main advantages
- Use the scikit-learn API
- Perform data preprocessing
- Explain the difference between supervised and unsupervised models, as well as the importance of choosing the right algorithm for each dataset

This chapter gives an explanation of the scikit-learn syntax and features in order to be able to process and visualize data

Introduction

Scikit-learn is a well-documented and easy-to-use library that facilitates the application of machine learning algorithms by using simple methods, which ultimately enables beginners to model data without the need for deep knowledge of the math behind the algorithms. Additionally, thanks to the ease of use of this library, it allows the user to implement different approximations (create different models) for a data problem. Moreover, by removing the task of coding the algorithm, scikit-learn allows teams to focus their attention on analyzing the results of the model to arrive at crucial conclusions.

Spotify, a world leading company in the field of music streaming, uses scikit-learn, since it allows them to implement multiple models for a data problem, which are then easily connectable to their existing development. This process improves the process of arriving at a useful model, while allowing the company to plug them into their current app with little effort.

On the other hand, booking.com uses scikit-learn due to the wide variety of algorithms that the library offers, which allows them to fulfill the different data analysis tasks that the company relies on, such as building recommendation engines, detecting fraudulent activities, and managing the customer service team.

Considering the preceding points, this chapter begins with an explanation of scikit-learn and its main uses and advantages, and then moves on to provide a brief explanation of the scikit-learn API syntax and features. Additionally, the process to represent, visualize, and normalize data is shown. The aforementioned information will be useful to understand the different steps taken to develop a machine learning model.

Scikit-Learn

Created in 2007 by David Cournapeau as part of a Google Summer of Code project, scikit-learn is an open source Python library made to facilitate the process of building models based on built-in machine learning and statistical algorithms, without the need for hard-coding. The main reasons for its popular use are its complete documentation, its easy-to-use API, and the many collaborators who work every day to improve the library.

> **Note**
>
> You can find the documentation for scikit-learn at the following link: http://scikit-learn.org.

Scikit-learn is mainly used to model data, and not as much to manipulate or summarize data. It offers its users an easy-to-use, uniform API to apply different models, with little learning effort, and no real knowledge of the math behind it, required.

> **Note**
>
> Some of the math topics that you need to know about to understand the models are linear algebra, probability theory, and multivariate calculus. For more information on these models, visit: https://towardsdatascience.com/the-mathematics-of-machine-learning-894f046c568.

The models available under the scikit-learn library fall into two categories: supervised and unsupervised, both of which will be explained in depth in later sections. This category classification will help to determine which model to use for a particular dataset to get the most information out of it.

Besides its main use for interpreting data to train models, scikit-learn is also used to do the following:

- Perform predictions, where new data is fed to the model to predict an outcome
- Carry out cross validation and performance metrics analysis to understand the results obtained from the model, and thereby improve its performance
- Obtain sample datasets to test algorithms over them
- Perform feature extraction to extract features from images or text data

Although scikit-learn is considered the preferred Python library for beginners in the world of machine learning, there are several large companies around the world using it, as it allows them to improve their product or services by applying the models to already existing developments. It also permits them to quickly implement tests over new ideas.

> **Note**
>
> You can visit the following website to find out which companies are using scikit-learn and what are they using it for: http://scikit-learn.org/stable/testimonials/testimonials.html.

In conclusion, scikit-learn is an open source Python library that uses an API to apply most machine learning tasks (both supervised or unsupervised) to data problems. Its main use is for modeling data; nevertheless, it should not be limited to that, as the library also allows users to predict outcomes based on the model being trained, as well as to analyze the performance of the model.

Advantages of Scikit-Learn

The following is a list of the main advantages of using scikit-learn for machine learning purposes:

- *Ease of use*: Scikit-learn is characterized by a clean API, with a small learning curve in comparison to other libraries such as TensorFlow or Keras. The API is popular for its uniformity and straightforward approach. Users of scikit-learn do not necessarily need to understand the math behind the models.
- *Uniformity*: Its uniform API makes it very easy to switch from model to model, as the basic syntax required for one model is the same for others.
- *Documentation/Tutorials*: The library is completely backed up by documentation, which is effortlessly accessible and easy to understand. Additionally, it also offers step-by-step tutorials that cover all of the topics required to develop any machine learning project.
- *Reliability and Collaborations*: As an open source library, scikit-learn benefits from the inputs of multiple collaborators who work each day to improve its performance. This participation from many experts from different contexts helps to develop not only a more complete library but also a more reliable one.
- *Coverage*: As you scan the list of components that the library has, you will discover that it covers most machine learning tasks, ranging from supervised models such as classification and regression algorithms to unsupervised models such as clustering and dimensionality reduction. Moreover, due to its many collaborators, new models tend to be added in relatively short amounts of time.

Disadvantages of Scikit-Learn

The following is a list of the main disadvantages of using scikit-learn for machine learning purposes:

- *Inflexibility*: Due to its ease of use, the library tends to be inflexible. This means that users do not have much liberty in parameter tuning or model architecture. This becomes an issue as beginners move to more complex projects.

- *Not Good for Deep Learning*: As mentioned previously, the performance of the library falls short when tackling complex machine learning projects. This is especially true for deep learning, as scikit-learn does not support deep neural networks with the necessary architecture or power.

In general terms, scikit-learn is an excellent beginner's library as it requires little effort to learn its use and has many complementary materials thought to facilitate its application. Due to the contributions of several collaborators, the library stays up to date and is applicable to most current data problems.

On the other hand, it is a fairly simple library, not fit for more complex data problems such as deep learning. Likewise, it is not recommended for users who wish to take its abilities to a higher level by playing with the different parameters that are available in each model.

Data Representation

The main objective of machine learning is to build models by interpreting data. To do so, it is highly important to feed the data in a way that is readable by the computer. To feed data into a scikit-learn model, it must be represented as a table or matrix of the required dimension, which will be discussed in the following section.

Tables of Data

Most tables fed into machine learning problems are two-dimensional, meaning that they contain rows and columns. Conventionally, each row represents an observation (an instance), whereas each column represents a characteristic (feature) of each observation.

The following table is a fragment of a sample dataset of scikit-learn. The purpose of the dataset is to differentiate from among three types of iris plants based on their characteristics. Hence, in the table, each row embodies a plant and each column denotes the value of that feature for every plant:

	sepal_length	sepal_width	petal_length	petal_width
0	5.1	3.5	1.4	0.2
1	4.9	3.0	1.4	0.2
2	4.7	3.2	1.3	0.2
3	4.6	3.1	1.5	0.2
4	5.0	3.6	1.4	0.2
5	5.4	3.9	1.7	0.4
6	4.6	3.4	1.4	0.3
7	5.0	3.4	1.5	0.2
8	4.4	2.9	1.4	0.2
9	4.9	3.1	1.5	0.1

Figure 1.1: A table showing the first 10 instances of the iris dataset

From the preceding explanation, the following snapshot shows data that corresponds to a plant with sepal length of 5.1, sepal width of 3.5, petal length of 1.4, and petal width of 0.2. The plant belongs to the **setosa** species:

	sepal_length	sepal_width	petal_length	petal_width	species
0	5.1	3.5	1.4	0.2	setosa

Figure 1.2: The first instance of the iris dataset

Note

When feeding images to a model, the tables become three-dimensional, where the rows and columns represent the dimensions of the image in pixels, while the depth represents its color scheme. If you are interested, feel free to explore more on the subject of *convolutional neural networks*.

Features and Target Matrices

For many data problems, one of the features of your dataset will be used as a **label**. This means that out of all the other features, this one is the target to which the model should generalize the data. For example, in the preceding table, we might choose the species as the target feature, and so we would like the model to find patterns based on the other features to determine whether a plant belongs to the `setosa` species. Therefore, it is important to learn how to separate the target matrix from the features matrix.

Features Matrix: The features matrix comprises data from each instance for all features, except the target. It can be either created using a NumPy array or a Pandas DataFrame, and its dimensions are `[n_i, n_f]`, where `n_i` denotes the number of instances (such as a person) and `n_f` denotes the number of features (such as age). Generally, the features matrix is stored in a variable named `X`.

Target Matrix: Different than the features matrix, the target matrix is usually one-dimensional since it only carries one feature for all instances, meaning that its length is of value `n_i` (number of instances). Nevertheless, there are some occasions where multiple targets are required, and so the dimensions of the matrix become `[n_i, n_t]`, where `n_t` is the number of targets to consider.

Similar to the features matrix, the target matrix is usually created as a NumPy array or a Pandas series. The values of the target array may be discrete or continuous. Generally, the target matrix is stored in a variable named `Y`.

Exercise 1: Loading a Sample Dataset and Creating the Features and Target Matrices

> **Note**
>
> All of the exercises and activities in these chapters will be primarily developed in Jupyter Notebook. It is recommended to keep a separate notebook for different assignments, unless advised otherwise. Also, to load a sample dataset, the seaborn library will be used, as it displays the data as a table. Other ways to load data will be explained in further sections.

In this exercise, we will be loading the **iris** dataset, and creating features and target matrices using this dataset.

> **Note**
>
> For the exercises and activities within this chapter, you will need to have Python 3.6, seaborn, Jupyter, Matplotlib, and Pandas installed on your system.

1. Open a Jupyter Notebook to implement this exercise. In the cmd or terminal, navigate to the desired path and use the following command: **jupyter notebook**.
2. Load the **iris** dataset using the seaborn library. To do so, you first need to import the seaborn library, and then use the **load_dataset()** function, as shown in the following code:

```
import seaborn as sns
iris = sns.load_dataset('iris')
```

   As we can see from the preceding code, after importing the library, a nickname is given to facilitate its use along with the script.

   The **load_dataset()** function loads datasets from an online repository. The data from the dataset is stored in a variable named **iris**.

3. Create a variable, **X**, to store the features. Use the **drop()** function to include all of the features but the target, which in this case is named **species**. Then, print out the top 10 instances of the variable:

```
X = iris.drop('species', axis=1)
X.head(10)
```

> **Note**
>
> The axis parameter in the preceding snippet denotes whether you want to drop the label from rows (axis = 0) or columns (axis = 1).

The printed output should look as follows:

	sepal_length	sepal_width	petal_length	petal_width
0	5.1	3.5	1.4	0.2
1	4.9	3.0	1.4	0.2
2	4.7	3.2	1.3	0.2
3	4.6	3.1	1.5	0.2
4	5.0	3.6	1.4	0.2
5	5.4	3.9	1.7	0.4
6	4.6	3.4	1.4	0.3
7	5.0	3.4	1.5	0.2
8	4.4	2.9	1.4	0.2
9	4.9	3.1	1.5	0.1

Figure 1.3: A table showing the first 10 instances of the features matrix

4. Print the shape of your new variable using the **X.shape** command:

```
X.shape
(150, 4)
```

The first value indicates the number of instances in the dataset (150), and the second value represents the number of features (4).

5. Create a variable, **Y**, that will store the target values. There is no need to use a function for this. Use indexing to grab only the desired column. Indexing allows you to access a section of a larger element. In this case, we want to grab the column named **species**. Then, print out the top 10 values of the variable:

```
Y = iris['species']
Y.head(10)
```

The printed output should look as follows:

```
0    setosa
1    setosa
2    setosa
3    setosa
4    setosa
5    setosa
6    setosa
7    setosa
8    setosa
9    setosa
Name: species, dtype: object
```

Figure 1.4: A screenshot showing the first 10 instances of the target matrix

6. Print the shape of your new variable by using the **Y.shape** command:

   ```
   Y.shape
   (150,)
   ```

   The shape should be one-dimensional with length equal to the number of instances (150).

Congratulations! You have successfully created the features and target matrices of a dataset.

Generally, the preferred way to represent data is by using two-dimensional tables, where the rows represent the number of observations, also known as instances, and the columns represent the characteristics of those instances, commonly known as features.

For data problems that require target labels, the data table needs to be partitioned into a features matrix and a target matrix. The features matrix will contain the values of all features but the target, for each instance, making it a two-dimensional matrix. On the other hand, the target matrix will only contain the value of the target feature for all entries, making it a one-dimensional matrix.

Activity 1: Selecting a Target Feature and Creating a Target Matrix

In this activity, we will attempt to load a dataset and create the features and target matrices by choosing the appropriate target feature for the objective of the study. Let's look at the following scenario: you work in the safety department of a cruise company. The company wants to include more lower-deck cabins, but it wants to be sure that the measure will not increase the number of fatalities in the case of an accident.

The company has provided your team with a dataset of the Titanic passenger list to determine whether lower-deck passengers are less likely to survive. Your job is to select the target feature that most likely helps to achieve this objective.

> **Note**
>
> To choose the target feature, remember that the target should be the outcome to which we want to interpret the data for. For instance, if we want to know what features play a role in determining a plant's species, the species should be the target value.

Follow the steps below to complete this activity:

1. Load the **titanic** dataset using the **seaborn** library. The first couple of rows should look like this:

	survived	pclass	sex	age	sibsp	parch	fare	embarked	class	who	adult_male	deck	embark_town	alive	alone
0	0	3	male	22.0	1	0	7.2500	S	Third	man	True	NaN	Southampton	no	False
1	1	1	female	38.0	1	0	71.2833	C	First	woman	False	C	Cherbourg	yes	False
2	1	3	female	26.0	0	0	7.9250	S	Third	woman	False	NaN	Southampton	yes	True
3	1	1	female	35.0	1	0	53.1000	S	First	woman	False	C	Southampton	yes	False
4	0	3	male	35.0	0	0	8.0500	S	Third	man	True	NaN	Southampton	no	True
5	0	3	male	NaN	0	0	8.4583	Q	Third	man	True	NaN	Queenstown	no	True
6	0	1	male	54.0	0	0	51.8625	S	First	man	True	E	Southampton	no	True
7	0	3	male	2.0	3	1	21.0750	S	Third	child	False	NaN	Southampton	no	False
8	1	3	female	27.0	0	2	11.1333	S	Third	woman	False	NaN	Southampton	yes	False
9	1	2	female	14.0	1	0	30.0708	C	Second	child	False	NaN	Cherbourg	yes	False

Figure 1.5: An table showing the first 10 instances of the Titanic dataset

2. Select your preferred target feature for the goal of this activity.
3. Create both the features matrix and the target matrix. Make sure that you store the data from the features matrix in a variable, **X**, and the data from the target matrix in another variable, **Y**.

4. Print out the shape of each of the matrices, which should match the following values:

   Features matrix: (891,14)

   Target matrix: (891)

> **Note**
>
> The solution for this activity can be found on page 178.

Data Preprocessing

For the computer to be able to understand the data proficiently, it is necessary to not only feed the data in a standardized way but also make sure that the data does not contain outliers or noisy data, or even missing entries. This is important because failing to do so might result in the system making assumptions that are not true to the data. This will cause the model to train at a slower pace and to be less accurate due to misleading interpretations of data.

Moreover, data preprocessing does not end there. Models do not work the same way, and each one makes different assumptions. This means that we need to preprocess in terms of the model that is going to be used. For example, some models accept only numerical data, whereas others work with nominal and numerical data.

To achieve better results during data preprocessing, a good practice is to transform (preprocess) the data in different ways, and then test the different transformations in different models. That way, you will be able to select the right transformation for the right model.

Messy Data

Data that is missing information or that contains outliers or noise is considered to be **messy data**. Failing to perform any preprocessing to transform the data can lead to poorly created models of the data, due to the introduction of bias and information loss. Some of the issues with data that should be avoided will be explained here.

Missing Values

Features where a few instances have values, as well as instances where there are no values for any feature, are considered **missing data**. As you can see from the following image, the vertical red rectangle represents a feature with only 3 values out of 10, and the horizontal rectangle represents an instance with no values at all:

ID	Feature 1	Feature 2	Feature 3	Feature 4	Feature 5	Feature 6	Feature 7	Feature 8
id1		1	3	5	6	8	1	1
id2	4	5	2	6	7	2	1	3
id3	2		7	5	9	8	1	2
id4	1	2	7	5	2	1	6	3
id5	5	8	4	4	6	7	8	5
id6	4	5	9	1	3	4	6	4
id7	7	6	5		4	8	6	5
id8								6
id9	8	2	3	1	2	4	5	3
id10	4	5	92	6	4	9	7	7

Figure 1.6: An image that displays an instance with no values for any of the features, which makes it useless, and a feature with 7 missing values out of the 10 instances

Conventionally, a feature missing more than 5 to 10% of its values is considered to be missing data, and so needs to be dealt with. On the other hand, all instances that have missing values for all features should be eliminated as they do not provide any information to the model, and, on the contrary, may end up introducing bias.

When dealing with a feature with a high absence rate, it is recommended to either eliminate it or fill it with values. The most popular ways to replace the missing values are as follows:

- **Mean imputation**: Replacing missing values with the mean or median of the features' available values
- **Regression imputation**: Replacing missing values with the predicted values obtained from a regression function

While mean imputation is a simpler approach to implement, it may introduce bias as it evens out all instances in that matter. On the other hand, even though the regression approach matches the data to its predicted value, it may end up overfitting the model as all values introduced follow a function.

Lastly, when the missing values are found in a text feature such as gender, the best book of action would be to either eliminate them or replace them with a class labeled *uncategorized* or something similar. This is mainly because it is not possible to apply either mean or regression imputation over text.

Labeling missing values with a new category (*uncategorized*) is mostly done when eliminating them removes an important part of the dataset, and hence is not an appropriate book of action. In this case, even though the new label may have an effect on the model depending on the rationale used to label the missing values, leaving them empty is an even worse alternative as it causes the model to make assumptions on its own.

> **Note**
>
> To learn more on how to detect and handle missing values, feel free to visit the following page: https://towardsdatascience.com/how-to-handle-missing-data-8646b18db0d4.

Outliers

Outliers are values that are far from the mean. This means that if the values from an attribute follow a Gaussian distribution, the outliers are located at the tails.

Outliers can be global or local. The former group represents those values that are far from the entire set of values of a feature. For example, when analyzing data from all members of a neighborhood, a global outlier would be a person who is 180 years old (as shown in the following diagram (**A**)). The latter, on the other hand, represents values that are far from a subgroup of values of that feature. For the same example that we saw previously, a local outlier would be a college student who is 70 years old (**B**), which would normally differ from other college students in that neighborhood:

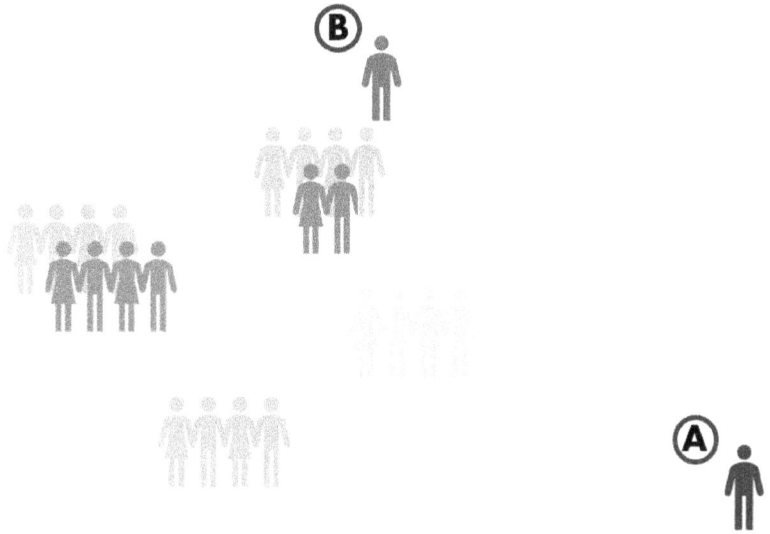

Figure 1.7: An image depicting global and local outliers in a dataset

Considering both examples that have been given, outliers do not evaluate whether the value is possible. While a person aged 180 years is not plausible, a 70-year-old college student might be a possibility, yet both are categorized as outliers as they can both affect the performance of the model.

A straightforward approach to detect outliers consists of visualizing the data to determine whether it follows a Gaussian distribution, and if it does, classifying those values that fall between three to six standard deviations away from the mean as outliers. Nevertheless, there is not an exact rule to determine an outlier, and the decision to select the number of standard deviations is subjective and will vary from problem to problem.

For example, if the dataset is reduced by 40% by setting three standard deviations as the parameter to rule out values, it would be appropriate to change the number of standard deviations to four.

On the other hand, when dealing with text features, detecting outliers becomes even trickier as there are no standard deviations to use. In this case, counting the occurrences of each class value would help to determine whether a certain class is indispensable or not. For instance, in clothing sizes, having a size XXS that represents less than 5% of the entire dataset might not be necessary.

Once the outliers are detected, there are three common ways to handle them:

- **Delete the outlier**: For outliers that are true values, it is best to completely delete them to avoid skewing the analysis. This may be a good idea for outliers that are mistakes, if the number of outliers is too large to perform further analysis to assign a new a value.
- **Define a top**: Defining a top might also be useful for true values. For instance, if you realize that all values above a certain threshold behave the same way, you can consider topping that value with the threshold.
- **Assign a new value**: If the outlier is clearly a mistake, you can assign a new value using one of the techniques that we discussed for missing values (mean or regression imputation).

The decision to use each of the preceding approaches depends on the outlier type and number. Most of the time, if the number of outliers represents a small proportion of the total size of the dataset, there is no point in treating the outlier in any way other than deleting it.

> **Note**
>
> Noisy data corresponds to values that are not correct or possible. This includes numerical (outliers that are mistakes) and nominal values (for example, a person's gender misspelled as "fimale"). Like outliers, noisy data can be treated by deleting the values completely or by assigning them a new value.

Exercise 2: Dealing with Messy Data

In this exercise, we will be using the **titanic** dataset as an example to demonstrate how to deal with messy data:

1. Open a Jupyter Notebook to implement this exercise.
2. Load the **titanic** dataset and store it in a variable called **titanic**. Use the following code:

```
import seaborn as sns
titanic = sns.load_dataset('titanic')
```

3. Next, create a variable called **age** to store the values of that feature from the dataset. Print out the top 10 values of the **age** variable:

```
age = titanic['age']
age.head(10)
```

The output will appear as follows:

```
0    22.0
1    38.0
2    26.0
3    35.0
4    35.0
5     NaN
6    54.0
7     2.0
8    27.0
9    14.0
Name: age, dtype: float64
```

Figure 1.8: A screenshot showing the first 10 instances of the age variable

As you can see, the feature has **NaN** (**Not a Number**) values, which represent missing values.

4. Check the shape of the **age** variable. Then, count the number of **NaN** values to determine how to handle them. Use the **isnull()** function to find the **NaN** values, and use the **sum()** function to sum them all:

```
age.shape
(891,)
age.isnull().sum()
177
```

5. The participation of the **NaN** values in the total size of the variable is 5.03%. Although this is not high enough to consider removing the entire feature, there is a need to handle the missing values.

6. Let's choose the mean imputation methodology to replace the missing values. To do so, compute the mean of the available values. Use the following code:

```
mean = age.mean()
mean = mean.round()
mean
```

The mean comes to be 30.

> **Note**
>
> The value was rounded to its nearest integer since we are dealing with age.

7. Replace all missing values with the mean. Use the **fillna()** function. To check that the values have been replaced, print the first ten values again:

```
age.fillna(mean,inplace=True)
age.head(10)
```

> **Note**
>
> Set **inplace** to **True** to replace the values in the places where the **NaN** values are.

The printed output is shown below:

```
0    22.0
1    38.0
2    26.0
3    35.0
4    35.0
5    30.0
6    54.0
7     2.0
8    27.0
9    14.0
Name: age, dtype: float64
```

Figure 1.9: A screenshot depicting the first 10 instances of the age variable

As you can see in the preceding screenshot, the age of the instance with index 5 has changed from **NaN** to 30, which is the mean that was calculated previously. The same procedure occurs for all 177 **NaN** values.

8. Import Matplotlib and graph a histogram of the **age** variable. Use Matplotlib's **hist() function**. To do so, type in the following code:

```
import matplotlib.pyplot as plt
plt.hist(age)
plt.show()
```

The histogram should look like it does in the following diagram, and as we can see, its distribution is Gaussian-like:

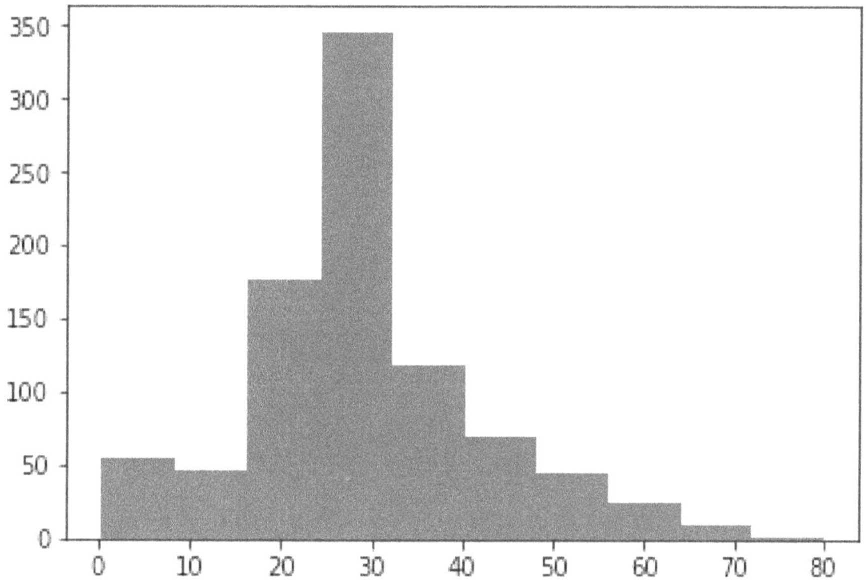

Figure 1.10: A screenshot depicting the histogram of the age variable

9. Discover the outliers in the data. Let's use three standard deviations as the measure to calculate the min and max values.

As discussed previously, the min value is determined by calculating the mean of all of the values and subtracting three standard deviations from it. Use the following code to set the min value and store it in a variable named **min_val**:

```
min_val = age.mean() - (3 * age.std())
min_val
```

The min value comes to be around −9.248. According to the min value, there are no outliers at the left tail of the Gaussian distribution. This makes sense, given that the distribution is tilted slightly to the left.

Opposite to the min value, for the max value, the standard deviations are added to the mean to calculate the higher threshold. Calculate the max value, as shown in the following code, and store it in a variable named **max_val**:

```
max_val = age.mean() + (3 * age.std())
max_val
```

The max value, which comes to around 68.766, determines that instances with ages above 68.76 years represent outliers. As you can see in the preceding diagram, this also makes sense as there are little instances over that threshold and they are in fact far away from the bell of the Gaussian distribution.

10. Count the number of instances that are above the max value to decide how to handle them.

First, using indexing, call the values in **age** that are above the max value, and store them in a variable called outliers. Then, count the outliers using **count()**:

```
outliers = age[age > max_val]
outliers.count()
```

The output shows us that there are seven outliers. Print out the outliers by typing in **outliers** and check that the correct values were stored:

```
96     71.0
116    70.5
493    71.0
630    80.0
672    70.0
745    70.0
851    74.0
Name: age, dtype: float64
```

Figure 1.11: A screenshot depicting the outliers

As the number of outliers is small, and they correspond to true outliers, they can be deleted.

> **Note**
>
> For this exercise, we will be deleting the instances from the **age** variable to understand the complete procedure of dealing with outliers. However, later, the deletion of outliers will be handled in consideration of all features, in order to delete the entire instance, and not just the age values.

11. Redefine the value stored in **age** by using indexing to include only values below the max threshold. Then, print the shape of **age**:

```
age = age[age <= max_val]
age.shape
(884,)
```

As you can see, the shape of **age** has been reduced by seven, which was the number of outliers.

Congratulations! You have successfully cleaned out a Pandas Series. This process serves as a guide for cleaning a dataset later on.

To summarize, we have discussed the importance of preprocessing data, as failing to do so may introduce bias in the model, which affects the training time of the model and its performance. Some of the main forms of messy data are missing values, outliers, and noise.

Missing values, as their name suggests, are those values that are left empty or null. When dealing with many missing values, it is important to handle them by deletion or by assigning new values. Two ways to assign new values were also discussed: mean imputation and regression imputation.

Outliers are values that fall far from the mean of all the values of a feature. One way to detect outliers is by selecting all the values that fall outside the mean minus/plus three-six standard deviations. Outliers may be mistakes (values that are not possible) or true values, and they should be handled differently. While true outliers may be deleted or topped, mistakes should be replaced with other values when possible.

Finally, noisy data corresponds to values that are, regardless of their proximity to the mean, mistakes or typos in the data. They can be of numeric, ordinal, or nominal types.

> **Note**
>
> Please remember that numeric data is always represented by numbers that can be measured, nominal data refers to text data that does not follow a rank, and ordinal data refers to text data that follows a rank or order.

Dealing with Categorical Features

Categorical features are those that comprise discrete values typically belonging to a finite set of categories. Categorical data can be nominal or ordinal. Nominal refers to categories that do not follow a specific order, such as music genre or city names, whereas ordinal refers to categories with a sense of order, such as clothing sizes or level of education.

Feature Engineering

Even though improvements in many machine learning algorithms have enabled the algorithms to understand categorical data types such as text, the process of transforming them into numeric values facilitates the training process of the model, which results in faster running times and better performance. This is mainly due to the elimination of semantics available in each category, as well as the fact that the conversion into numeric values allows you to scale all of the features of the dataset equally, as explained previously.

How does it work? Feature engineering generates a label encoding that assigns a numeric value to each category; this value will then replace the category in the dataset. For example, a variable called **genre** with the classes pop, rock, and country can be converted as follows:

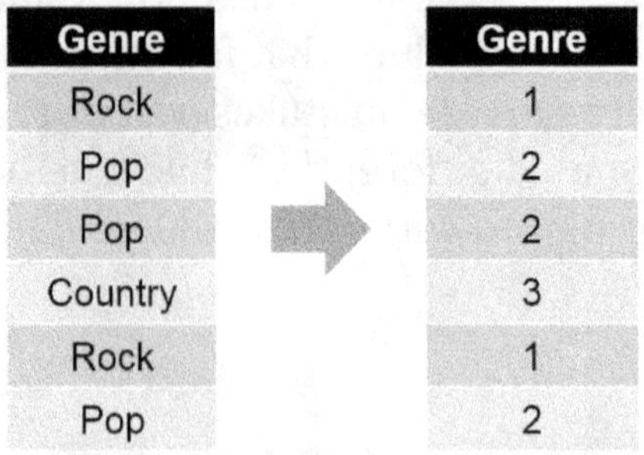

Figure 1.12: An image illustrating how feature engineering works

Exercise 3: Applying Feature Engineering over Text Data

In this exercise, we will be converting the text data within the **embark_town** feature of the **titanic** dataset into numerical data. Follow these steps:

1. Use the same Jupyter Notebook that you created for the last exercise.
2. Import scikit-learn's **LabelEncoder()** class, as well as the Pandas library. Use the following code:

```
from sklearn.preprocessing import LabelEncoder
import pandas as pd
```

3. Create a variable called **em_town** and store the information of that feature from the **titanic** dataset that was imported in the previous exercise. Print the top 10 values from the new variable:

```
em_town = titanic['embark_town']
em_town.head(10)
```

The output looks as follows:

```
0    Southampton
1      Cherbourg
2    Southampton
3    Southampton
4    Southampton
5     Queenstown
6    Southampton
7    Southampton
8    Southampton
9      Cherbourg
Name: embark_town, dtype: object
```

Figure 1.13: A screenshot depicting the first 10 instances of the em_town variable

As you can see, the variable contains text data.

4. Convert the text data into numeric values. Use the class that was imported previously (**LabelEncoder**):

```
enc = LabelEncoder()
new_label = pd.Series(enc.fit_transform(em_town.astype('str')))
```

First of all, initialize the class by typing in the first line of code. Second, create a new variable called **new_label** and use the built-in method **fit_transform()** from the class, which will assign a numeric value to each category and output the result. We use the **pd.Series()** function to convert the output from the label encoder into a Pandas Series. Print out the top 10 values of the new variable:

```
new_label.head(10)
```

```
0    2
1    0
2    2
3    2
4    2
5    1
6    2
7    2
8    2
9    0
dtype: int64
```

Figure 1.14: A screenshot depicting the first 10 instances of the **new_label** variable

As you can see, the text categories of the variable have been converted into numeric values.

Congratulations! You have successfully converted text data into numeric values.

While improvements in machine learning have made dealing with text features easier for some algorithms, it is best to convert them into numeric values. This is mainly important as it eliminates the complexity of dealing with semantics, not to mention that it gives the flexibility to change from model to model, without any limitations.

Text data conversion is done via feature engineering, where every text category is assigned a numeric value that replaces it. Furthermore, even though this can be done manually, there are powerful built-in classes and methods that facilitate this process. One example of this is the use of scikit-learn's **LabelEncoder** class.

Rescaling Data

Why is it important to rescale data? Because even though the data may be fed to a model using different scales for each feature, the lack of homogeneity can cause the algorithm to lose its ability to discover patterns from the data due to the assumptions it has to make to understand it, thereby slowing down the training process and negatively affecting the model's performance.

Data rescaling helps the model run faster, without any burden or responsibility to learn from the invariance present in the dataset. Moreover, a model trained over equally scaled data assigns the same weights to all parameters, which allows the algorithm to generalize to all features and not just to those with higher values, irrespective of their meaning.

An example of a dataset with different scales is one that contains different features, one measured in kilograms, another measuring temperature, and another counting the number of children. Even though the values of each attribute are true, the scale of each one of them highly differs from that of the other. For example, while the values in kilograms can go higher than 100, the children count will typically not go further than 10.

Two of the most popular ways to rescale data are data normalization and data standardization. There is no rule on selecting the methodology to transform data to scale it, as all datasets behave differently. The best practice is to transform the data using two or three rescaling methodologies and test the algorithms in each one of them in order to choose the one that best fits the data based on the performance.

Rescaling methodologies are to be used individually. When testing different rescaling methodologies, the transformation of data should be done independently. Each transformation can be tested over a model, and the best suited one should be chosen for further steps.

Normalization: Data normalization in machine learning consists of rescaling the values of all features such that they lie in a range between 0 and 1 and have a maximum length of one. This serves the purpose of equating attributes of different scales.

The following equation allows you to normalize the values of a feature:

$$z_i = \frac{x_i - \min(x)}{\max(x) - \min(x)}$$

Figure 1.15: The normalization equation

Here, *zi* corresponds to the *ith* normalized value and *x* represents all values.

Standardization: This is a rescaling technique that transforms the data into a Gaussian distribution with a mean equal to 0 and a standard deviation equal to 1.

One simple way of standardizing a feature is shown in the following equation:

$$z_i = \frac{x_i - mean(x)}{std(x)}$$

Figure 1.16: The standardization equation

Here, *zi* corresponds to the *ith* standardized value, and *x* represents all values.

Exercise 4: Normalizing and Standardizing Data

This section covers the normalization and standardization of data, using the **titanic** dataset as an example. Use the same Jupyter Notebook that you created for the last exercise:

1. Using the **age** variable that was created in the first exercise of this notebook, normalize the data using the preceding formula and store it in a new variable called **age_normalized**. Print out the top 10 values:

```
age_normalized = (age - age.min())/(age.max()-age.min())
age_normalized.head(10)
```

```
0    0.329064
1    0.573041
2    0.390058
3    0.527295
4    0.527295
5    0.451052
6    0.817017
7    0.024093
8    0.405306
9    0.207075
Name: age, dtype: float64
```

Figure 1.17: A screenshot displaying the first 10 instances of the **age_normalized** variable

As you can see in the preceding screenshot, all of the values have been converted to their equivalents in a range between 0 and 1. By performing the normalization for all of the features, the model will be trained on the features of the same scale.

2. Again, using the **age** variable, standardize the data using the formula for standardization, and store it in a variable called **age_standardized**. Print out the top 10 values:

```
age_standardized = (age - age.mean())/age.std()
age_standardized.head(10)
```

```
0   -0.594548
1    0.687225
2   -0.274105
3    0.446892
4    0.446892
5    0.046338
6    1.968998
7   -2.196765
8   -0.193994
9   -1.235435
Name: age, dtype: float64
```

Figure 1.18: A screenshot displaying the first 10 instances of the **age_standardized** variable

Different than normalization, in standardization, the values distribute normally around zero.

3. Print out the mean and standard deviation of the **age_standardized** variable to confirm its mean of 0 and standard deviation of 1:

```
print("Mean: " + str(age_standardized.mean()))
print("Standard Deviation: " + str(age_standardized.std()))
Mean: 9.645376503530772e-17
Standard Deviation: 1.0
```

As you can see, the mean approximates to 0, and the standard deviation is equal to 1, which means that the standardization of the data was successful.

Congratulations! You have successfully applied rescaling methods to your data.

In conclusion, we have covered the final step in data preprocessing, which consists of rescaling data. This process was done in a dataset with features of different scales, with the objective of homogenizing the way data is represented to facilitate the comprehension of the data by the model.

Failing to rescale data will cause the model to train at a slower pace and might negatively affect the performance of the model.

Two methodologies for data rescaling were explained in this topic: normalization and standardization. On one hand, normalization transforms the data to a length of one (from 0 to 1). On the other hand, standardization converts the data into a Gaussian distribution with a mean of 0 and a standard deviation of 1.

Given that there is no rule for selecting the appropriate rescaling methodology, the recommended book of action is to transform the data using two or three rescaling methodologies independently, and then train the model with each transformation to evaluate the methodology that behaves best.

Activity 2: Preprocessing an Entire Dataset

You continue to work for the safety department at a cruise company. As you did great work selecting the ideal target feature to develop the study, the department has decided to commission you into preprocessing the data set as well. For this purpose, you need to use all the techniques you have learned about previously to preprocess the dataset and get it ready for model training. The following steps serve to guide you in that direction:

1. Load the dataset and create the features and target matrices by typing in the following code:

```
import seaborn as sns
titanic = sns.load_dataset('titanic')
X = titanic[['sex','age','fare','class','embark_town','alone']]
Y = titanic['survived']
```

> **Note**
>
> For this activity, the features matrix has been created using only six features, as some of the other features were redundant for the study. For example, there is no need to keep both **sex** and **gender**.

2. Check for missing values and outliers in all the features of the features matrix (**X**). Choose a methodology to handle them.

> **Note**
>
> The following functions might come in handy:
>
> **notnull()**: To detect non-missing values. For instance, **X[X["age"].notnull()]** will retrieve all the rows in X, except those that are missing values under the column **age**.
>
> **value.counts()**: To count the occurrence of unique values of an array. For example, **X["gender"].value_counts()** will count the number of times the classes **male** and **female** are present.

3. Convert all text features into its numeric representation.

> **Note**
>
> Use the **LabelEncoder** class from scikit-learn. Don't forget to initialize the class before calling any of its methods.

4. Rescale your data, either by normalizing or standardizing.

> **Note**
>
> The solution for this activity can be found on page 179.

Results may vary depending on the choices you made. However, you must be left with a dataset with no missing values, outliers, or text features, and with data rescaled.

Scikit-Learn API

The objective of the scikit-learn API is to provide an efficient and unified syntax to make machine learning accessible to non-machine learning experts, as well as to facilitate and popularize its use among several industries.

How Does It Work?

Although it has many collaborators, the scikit-learn API was built and has been updated by considering a set of principles that prevent framework code proliferation, where different codes perform similar functionalities. On the contrary, it promotes simple conventions and consistency. Due to this, the scikit-learn API is consistent among all models, and once the main functionalities have been learned, it can be widely used.

The scikit-learn API is divided into three complementary interfaces that share a common syntax and logic: the estimator, the predictor, and the transformer. The estimator interface is used for creating models and fitting the data into them; the predictor, as the name suggests, is used to make predictions based on the models trained before; and finally, the transformer is used for converting data.

Estimator

This is considered to be the core of the entire API, as it is the interface in charge of fitting the models to the input data. It works by initializing the model to be used, and then applying a **`fit()`** method that triggers the learning process to build a model based on the data.

The **`fit()`** method receives as arguments the training data, in two separate variables, the features matrix, and the target matrix (conventionally called **`X_train`** and **`Y_train`**). For unsupervised models, the method only takes in the first argument (**`X_train`**).

This method creates the model trained to the input data, which can later be used for predicting.

Some models take other arguments besides the training data, which are also called **hyperparameters**. These hyperparameters are initially set to their default values, but can be tuned to improve the performance of the model, which will be discussed in further sections.

The following is an example of a model being trained:

```
from sklearn.naive_bayes import GaussianNB

model = GaussianNB()

model.fit(X_train, Y_train)
```

First, it is required that you import the type of algorithm to be used from scikit-learn, for example, a Gaussian Naïve Bayes algorithm for classification. It is always a good practice to import only the algorithm to be used, and not the entire library, as this will ensure that your code runs faster.

> **Note**
>
> To find out the syntax to import a different model, use the documentation of scikit-learn. Go to the following link, click over the algorithm that you wish to implement, and you will find the instructions there: http://scikit-learn.org/stable/user_guide.html.

The second line of code oversees the initialization of the model and stores it in a variable. Lastly, the model is fit to the input data.

In addition to this, the estimator also offers other complementary tasks, as follows:

- Feature extraction, which involves transforming input data into numerical features that can be used for machine learning purposes
- Feature selection, which selects the features in your data that most contribute to the prediction output of the model
- Dimensionality reduction, which takes higher-dimensional data and converts it into a lower dimension

Predictor

As explained previously, the predictor takes the model created by the estimator and extends it to perform predictions on unseen data. In general terms, for supervised models, it feeds the model a new set of data, usually called **X_test**, to get a corresponding target or label based on the parameters learned during the training of the model.

Moreover, some unsupervised models can also benefit from the predictor. While this method does not output a specific target value, it can be useful to assign a new instance to a cluster.

Following the preceding example, the implementation of the predictor can be seen as follows:

```
Y_pred = model.predict(X_test)
```

We apply the **predict()** method to the previously trained model, and input the new data as an argument to the method.

In addition to predicting, the predictor can also implement methods that are in charge of quantifying the confidence of the prediction, also called the performance of the model. These confidence functions vary from model to model, but their main objective is to determine how far the prediction is from reality. This is done by taking an **X_test** with its corresponding **Y_test** and comparing it to the predictions made with the same **X_test**.

Transformer

As we saw previously, data is usually transformed before being fed to a model. Considering this, the API contains a **transform()** method that allows you to perform some preprocessing techniques.

It can be used both as a starting point to transform the input data of the model (**X_train**), as well as further along to modify data that will be fed to the model for predictions. This latter application is crucial to get accurate results, as it ensures that the new data follows the same distribution as the data used to train the model.

The following is an example of a transformer that normalizes the values of the training data:

```
from sklearn.preprocessing import StandardScaler
scaler = StandardScaler()
scaler.fit(X_train)
X_train = scaler.transform(X_train)
```

As you can see, after importing and initializing the transformer, it needs to be fit to the data to then effectively transform it:

```
X_test = scaler.transform(X_test)
```

The advantage of the transformer is that once it has been applied to the training dataset, it stores the values used for transforming the training data; this can be used to transform the test dataset to the same distribution.

In conclusion, we discussed one of the main benefits of using scikit-learn, which is its API. This API follows a consistent structure that makes it easy for non-experts to apply machine learning algorithms.

To model an algorithm on scikit-learn, the first step is to initialize the model class and fit it to the input data using an estimator, which is usually done by calling the **`fit()`** method of the class. Finally, once the model has been trained, it is possible to predict new values using the predictor by calling the **`predict()`** method of the class.

Additionally, scikit-learn also has a transformer interface that allows you to transform data as needed. This is useful for performing preprocessing methods over the training data, which can then be also used to transform the testing data to follow the same distribution.

Supervised and Unsupervised Learning

Machine learning is divided into two main categories: supervised and unsupervised learning.

Supervised Learning

Supervised learning consists of understanding the relation between a given set of features and a target value, also known as a label or class. For instance, it can be used for modeling the relationship between a person's demographic information and their ability to pay loans, as shown in the following table:

Age	Sex	Education level	Income level	Marital status	Previous loan paid
30	Female	College	$97.000	Single	Yes
53	Male	HIgh school	$80.000	Signle	No
26	Male	Masters	$157.000	Married	Yes
35	Female	None	$55.000	Married	No
44	Female	Undergrad	$122.000	Single	Yes

Figure 1.19: A table depicting the relationship between a person's demographic information and the ability to pay loans

Models trained to foresee these relationships can then be applied to predict labels for new data. As we can see from the preceding example, a bank that builds such a model can then input data from loan applicants to determine if they are likely to pay back the loan.

These models can be further divided into classification and regression tasks, which are explained as follows.

Classification tasks are used to build models out of data with discrete categories as labels; for instance, a classification task can be used to predict whether a person will pay a loan. You can have more than two discrete categories, such as predicting the ranking of a horse in a race, but they must be a finite number.

Most classification tasks output the prediction as the probability of an instance to belong to each output label. The assigned label is the one with the highest probability, as can be seen in the following diagram:

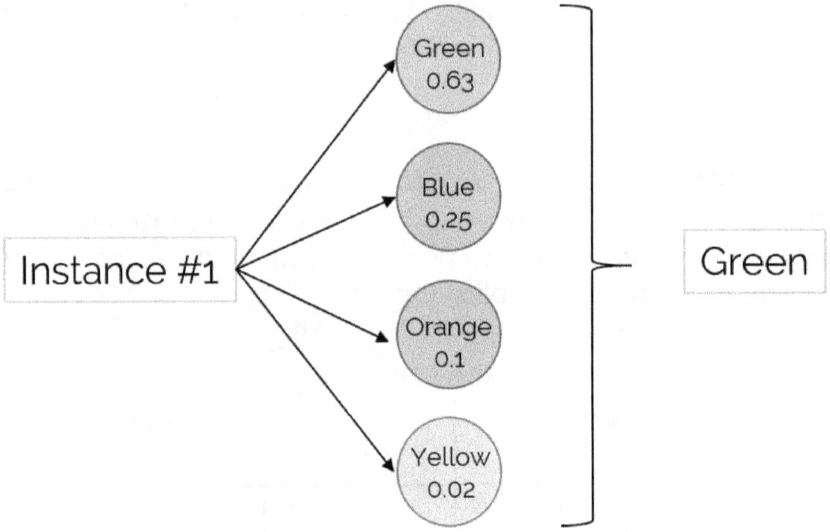

Figure 1.20: An illustration of the working of a classification algorithm

Some of the most common classification algorithms are as follows:

- **Decision trees**: This algorithm follows a tree-like architecture that simulates the decision process given a previous decision.
- **Naïve Bayes classifier**: This algorithm relies on a group of probabilistic equations based on Bayes' theorem, which assumes independence among features. It has the ability to consider several attributes.
- **Artificial neural networks (ANNs)**: These replicate the structure and performance of a biological neural network to perform pattern recognition tasks. An ANN consists of interconnected neurons, laid out with a set architecture. They pass information to one another until a result is achieved.

Regression tasks, on the other hand, are used for data with continuous quantities as labels; for example, a regression task can be used for predicting house prices. This means that the value is represented by a quantity and not by a set of possible outputs. Output labels can be of integer or float types:

- The most popular algorithm for regression tasks is **linear regression**. It consists of only one independent feature (x) whose relation with its dependent feature (y) is linear. Due to its simplicity, it is often overseen, even though it performs very well for simple data problems.
- Other, more complex regression algorithms include **regression trees** and **support vector regression**, as well as **ANNs** once again.

In conclusion, for supervised learning problems, each instance has a correct answer, also known as a label or class. The algorithms under this category aim to understand the data and then predict the class of a given set of features. Depending on the type of class (continuous or discrete), the supervised algorithms can be divided into classification or regression tasks.

Unsupervised Learning

Unsupervised learning consists of modeling the model to the data, without any relationship with an output label, also known as unlabeled data. This means that algorithms under this category search to understand the data and find patterns in it. For instance, unsupervised learning can be used to understand the profile of people belonging to a neighborhood, as shown in the following diagram:

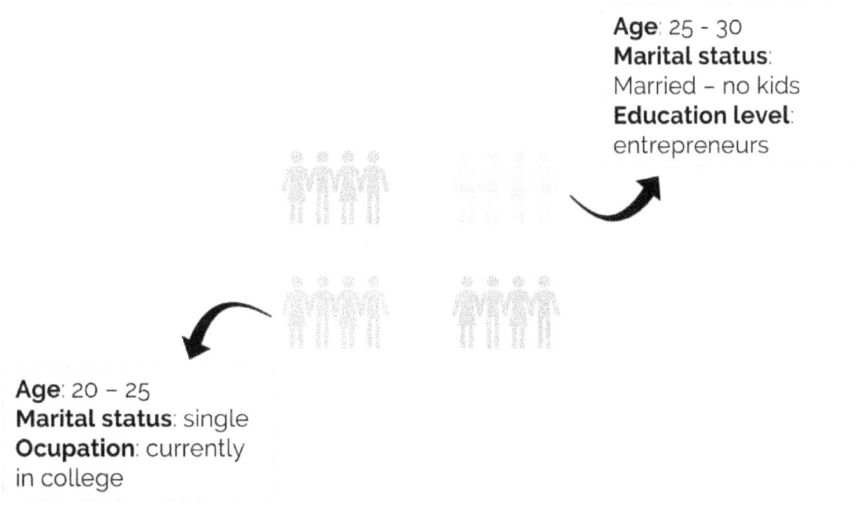

Figure 1.21: An illustration of how unsupervised algorithms can be used to understand the profiles of people

When applying a predictor over these algorithms, no target label is given as output. The prediction, only available for some models, consists of placing the new instance into one of the subgroups of data that has been created.

Unsupervised learning is further divided into different tasks, but the most popular one is clustering, which will be discussed next.

Clustering tasks involve creating groups of data (clusters) and complying with the condition that instances from other groups differ visibly from the instances within the group. The output of any clustering algorithm is a label, which assigns the instance to the cluster of that label:

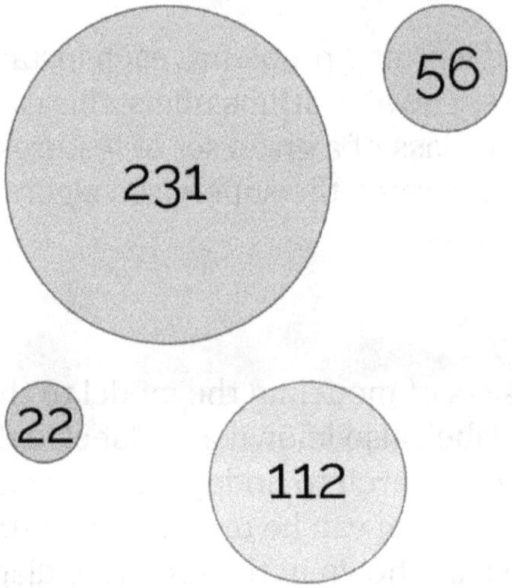

Figure 1.22: A diagram representing clusters of multiple sizes

The preceding diagram shows a group of clusters, each of a different size, based on the number of instances that belong to each cluster. Considering this, even though clusters do not need to have the same number of instances, it is possible to set the minimum number of instances per cluster to avoid overfitting the data into tiny clusters of very specific data.

Some of the most popular clustering algorithms are as follows:

- **k-means**: This focuses on separating the instances into n clusters of equal variance by minimizing the sum of the squared distances between two points.
- **Mean-shift clustering**: This creates clusters by using centroids. Each instance becomes a candidate for centroid to be the mean of the points in that cluster.
- **Density-Based Spatial Clustering of Applications with Noise (DBSCAN)**: This determines clusters as areas with a high density of points, separated by areas with low density.

In conclusion, unsupervised algorithms are designed to understand data when there is no label or class that indicates a correct answer for each set of features. The most common types of unsupervised algorithms are the clustering methods that allow you to classify a population into different groups.

Summary

Machine learning consists of constructing models, some of which are based on complicated mathematical concepts, to understand data. Scikit-learn is an open source Python library that is meant to facilitate the process of applying these models to data problems, without much complex math knowledge required.

This chapter first covered an important step in developing a data problem, that is, representing the data in a tabular manner. Then, the steps involved in the creation of features and target matrices, data preprocessing, and choosing an algorithm were also covered.

Finally, after selecting the type of algorithm that best suits the data problem, the construction of the model can begin through the use of the scikit-learn API, which has three interfaces: estimators, predictors, and transformers. Thanks to the uniformity of the API, learning to use the methods for one algorithm is enough to enable their use for others.

With all of this in mind, in the next chapter, we will focus on detailing the process of implementing an unsupervised algorithm to a real-life dataset.

2

Unsupervised Learning: Real-Life Applications

Learning Objectives

By the end of this chapter, you will be able to:

- Describe how clustering works
- Import and preprocess a dataset using Pandas and Matplotlib
- Explain the difference between the three clustering algorithms
- Solve an unsupervised learning data problem using different algorithms
- Compare the results of different algorithms to select the one with the best performance

This chapter describes a practical implementation of an unsupervised algorithm to a real-world dataset

Introduction

In the previous chapter, we saw how to represent data in a tabular format, create features and target matrices, preprocess data, and choose the algorithm that best suits the problem at hand. We also saw how the scikit-learn API works and why it is easy to use.

The main objective of this chapter is to solve a real-world case study, where the students will implement three different unsupervised learning solutions. These different applications serve to demonstrate the uniformity of the scikit-learn API, as well as to explain the steps taken to solve such a problem. At the end of this chapter, the students will be able to understand the use of unsupervised learning to comprehend data in order to make informed decisions.

Clustering

Clustering is a type of unsupervised machine-learning technique, where the objective is to arrive at conclusions based on the patterns found within unlabeled input data. This technique is mainly used to find meaning in the structure of large data in order to draw decisions.

For instance, from a large list of restaurants in a city, it would be useful to segregate the market into subgroups based on the type of food, quantity of clients, and style of experience to offer each cluster a service that's been configured to its specific needs.

Moreover, clustering algorithms divide the data points into *n* number of clusters so that the data points in the same cluster have similar features, whereas they greatly differ from the data points in other clusters.

Clustering Types

Clustering algorithms can classify data points using a methodology that is either **hard** or **soft**. The former designates data points completely to a cluster, whereas the latter method calculates for each data point the probability of belonging to each cluster.

For example, for a dataset containing customer's past orders that are divided into eight subgroups (clusters), hard clustering occurs when each customer is placed inside one of the eight clusters. On the other hand, soft clustering assigns each customer a probability of belonging to each of the eight clusters.

Considering that clusters are created based on the similarity between data points, clustering algorithms can be further divided into several groups depending on the set of rules used to measure similarity. Four of the most commonly known set of rules are explained as follows:

- **Connectivity-based models**: This model's approach to similarity is based on proximity in a data space. The creation of clusters can be done by assigning all data points to a single cluster, and then partitioning the data into smaller clusters as the distance between data points increases. Likewise, the algorithm can also start by assigning each data point an individual cluster, and then aggregating data points that are close by. An example of a connectivity-based model is hierarchical clustering.
- **Density-based models**: As the name indicates, these models define clusters by their density in the data space. This means that areas with a high density of data points will become clusters, which are typically separated from one another by low-density areas. An example of this is the DBSCAN algorithm.
- **Distribution-based models**: Models that fall in this category are based on the probability that all data points from a cluster follow the same distribution, such as a Gaussian distribution. An example of such a model is the expectation-maximization algorithm.
- **Centroid-based models**: These models are based on algorithms that define a centroid for each cluster, which is updated constantly by an iterative process. The data points are assigned to the cluster where their proximity to the centroid is minimized. An example of such a model is the k-means algorithm.

In conclusion, data points are assigned to clusters based on their similarity to each other and considering that they differ greatly from data points in other clusters. This classification into clusters can be either absolute or by determining the probability of each data point belonging to each cluster.

Moreover, there is no fixed set of rules to determine similarity between data points, which is why different clustering algorithms use different rules. Some of the most commonly known sets of rules are connectivity-based, density-based, distribution-based, and centroid-based.

Applications of Clustering

As with all machine-learning algorithms, clustering has many applications in different fields, some of which are explained as follows:

- **Search engine results**: Clustering can be used to generate search engine results containing keywords that are approximate to the keywords searched by the user and ordered as per the search result with greater similarity. Take Google as an example; it uses clustering segmentation not only for retrieving results, but also for suggesting new possible searches.

- **Recommendation programs**: It can also be used in recommendation programs that cluster together, for instance, people that fall into a similar profile, and then make recommendations based on the products that each member of the cluster has bought. Take Amazon, for example, which recommends more items based on your purchase history and the purchases of similar users.
- **Image recognition**: This is where clusters are used to group together images that are considered to be similar. For instance, Facebook uses clustering to help suggest who is present in a picture.
- **Market segmentation**: Clustering can also be used for market segmentation to divide a list of prospects or clients into subgroups, to provide a customized experience or product. For example, Adobe uses clustering analysis to segment customers, to target them differently by recognizing those who are more willing to spend money.

The preceding examples demonstrate that clustering algorithms can be used to solve different data problems in different industries, with the primary purpose of understanding large amounts of historical data that, in some cases, can be used to classify new instances.

Exploring a Dataset: Wholesale Customers Dataset

As part of the process of learning the behavior and applications of clustering algorithms, the following sections of this chapter will focus on solving a real-life data problem using the Wholesale Customers dataset, which is available at the UC Irvine Machine Learning Repository.

> **Note**
>
> The Wholesale Customers dataset is available for download, and will be used in this topic's activity. The process of downloading it will be explained during the activity. However, students should access the following link to understand the steps that are given: http://archive.ics.uci.edu/ml/datasets/Wholesale+customers.

Datasets in repositories may contain raw, partially preprocessed, or preprocessed data. To use any of these datasets, ensure that you read the specifications of the data available to understand the process that needs to be followed to model the data effectively.

Understanding the Dataset

The suggested steps to be followed to set the book of action for a data problem will be explained. Each step will be explained generically and will then be followed with an explanation of its application in the current case study (the Wholesale Customers dataset):

1. Considering that the dataset is obtained from an online repository, it is crucial to understand the way in which data is presented by the authors.

   The current dataset consists of a snippet of historical data of clients from a wholesale distributor. It contains a total of 440 instances (each row) and eight features (each column).

2. Next, it is important to determine the purpose of the study, which is dependent on the data available. Even though this might seem like a redundant statement, many data problems become problematic because the researcher does not have a clear view of the purpose of the study, and hence the preprocessing methodology, the model, and the performance metrics are wrongly chosen.

   The purpose of using clustering algorithms over the Wholesale Customers dataset is to understand the behavior of each customer. This will allow you to group customers with similar behaviors in one cluster. The behavior of a customer will be defined by how much they spent on each category of products, as well as the channel and the region where they bought products.

3. Subsequently, explore all the features that are available. This is mainly done for two reasons. First, to rule out features that are considered to be of low relevance based on the purpose of the study, and second, to understand the way the values are presented to determine some of the preprocessing techniques that may be needed.

The current case study has eight features, each one of which is considered to be relevant to the purpose of the study. Each feature is explained in the following table:

Variable	Meaning	Type	Relevance
FRESH	Annual spending* on Fresh products	Continuous	These features help to identify the combination of categories that sell together based on the spending
MILK	Annual spending* on Dairy	Continuous	
GROCERY	Annual spending* on Grocery products	Continuous	
FROZEN	Annual spending* on Frozen products	Continuous	
DETERGENTS_PAPER	Annual spending* on Detergents and paper	Continuous	
DELICATESSEN	Delicatessen products	Continuous	
CHANNEL	Customer's sales channel	Nominal**	Both features help define users based on their purchasing habits by region and sales channel
REGION	Customer's region	Nominal**	

* Annual spending measured in monetary units.
** The author of the dataset converted the nominal features into their numeric representation.

Figure 2.1: A table explaining each of the features in the case study

In the preceding table, no features are to be dismissed and nominal features have already been handled by the author of the dataset.

As a summary, the first thing to do when choosing a dataset or being handed one is to understand the characteristics visible at first glance, which involves recognizing the information available, then determining the purpose of the project, and finally revising the feature parameters to select those that will be part of the study. Post this, data visualization is used to continue to understand data, after which the data is preprocessed.

Data Visualization

Once data has been revised generically to ensure that it can be used for the desired purpose, it is time to load the dataset and use data visualization to further understand it. Data visualization is not a requirement for developing a machine-learning project, especially when dealing with datasets with hundreds or thousands of features. However, it has become an integral part of machine learning, mainly for visualizing the following:

- Specific features that are causing trouble (for example, those that contain many missing or outlier values) and to understand how to deal with them
- The results from the model, such as the clusters created or the number of predicted instances for each labeled category
- The performance of the model in order to see the behavior along different iterations

Its popularity in the tasks detailed previously is explained by the fact that the human brain processes information easily when it is presented as charts or graphs, which allows us to have a general understanding of the data. It also helps to identify areas that need attention, such as outliers.

Loading the Dataset Using Pandas

One way of storing a dataset to easily manage it is by using Pandas DataFrames. These work as two-dimensional size-mutable matrices with labeled axes. They facilitate the use of different Pandas functions to modify the dataset for preprocessing purposes.

Most datasets found in online repositories or gathered by companies for data analysis are saved in **CSV (comma-separated values)** files. CSV files are text files that display the data in the form of a table. Columns are separated by commas (,) and rows are on separate lines.

Loading a dataset stored in a CSV file and placing it into a DataFrame is extremely easy with the Pandas function `read_csv()`. It receives as input the path to your file, as shown in the following screenshot:

> **Note**
>
> When datasets are stored in different forms of files, such as in Excel or SQL databases, use the Pandas functions `read_xlsx()` or `read_sql()`, respectively.

```
In [1]: import pandas as pd

        file_path = "datasets/test.csv"
        data = pd.read_csv(file_path)

        print(type(data))

        <class 'pandas.core.frame.DataFrame'>
```

Figure 2.2: A screenshot showing the output of the **read.csv()** function

As shown in the preceding screenshot, the variable named **data** is of a Pandas DataFrame.

Visualization Tools

There are different open source visualization libraries available, from which Seaborn and Matplotlib stand out. In the previous chapter, Seaborn was used to load and display data; however, from this section onward, Matplotlib will be used as the visualization library. This is mainly because Seaborn is built on top of Matplotlib with the sole purpose of introducing a couple of plot types and to improve the format of the displays. Therefore, once you learn Matplotlib, you can also import Seaborn to improve the visual quality of your plots.

> **Note**
>
> For more information on the Seaborn library, visit the following link: https://seaborn.pydata.org/.

In general terms, Matplotlib is an easy-to-use Python library that prints 2D quality figures. For simple plotting, the **pyplot** model of the library will suffice.

Some of the most commonly used plot types are explained in the following table:

Plot type	Definition	Function*	Visual representation
Histograms	Display the distribution of continuous data	`plt.hist()`	
Scatter plots	Display values for 2 variables using Cartesian coordinates	`plt.scatter()`	
Bar charts	Represent variables using bars, with heights proportional to the values they represent	`plt.bar()`	
Pie charts	A circular representation that displays proportions	`plt.pie()`	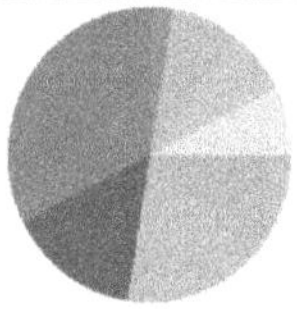

Figure 2.3: A table listing the commonly used plot types (*). The functions in the third column can be used after importing Matplotlib and its pyplot model.

> ### Note
>
> Access Matplotlib's documentation on the type of plot that you wish to use so that you can play around with the different arguments that you can use to edit the result of your plot.

Exercise 5: Plotting a Histogram of One Feature from the Noisy Circles Dataset

In this exercise, we will be plotting a histogram of one feature from the noisy circles dataset. Follow these steps to complete this exercise:

> **Note**
>
> Use the same Jupyter Notebook for all exercises and activities within this chapter.
>
> For all the exercises and activities within this chapter, you will need to have Python 3.6, Matplotlib, NumPy, Jupyter, and Pandas installed on your system.

1. Open a Jupyter Notebook to implement this exercise.
2. First, import all of the libraries that you are going to be using by typing the following code:

```
import pandas as pd
import numpy as np
import matplotlib.pyplot as plt
np.random.seed(0)
```

The Pandas library is used to save the dataset into a DataFrame, Matplotlib is used for visualization, and NumPy is used in later exercises of this chapter, but since the same notebook will be used, it is imported here.

> **Note**
>
> A numpy random seed is used to ensure that results obtained during the exercises of this chapter are consistent from run to run. Otherwise, they would change at every run due to the random initialization that occurs every time a model is trained.

3. Create the noisy circles dataset by using the scikit-learn utility **datasets**. Type in the following code:

```
from sklearn import datasets
n_samples = 1500
data = datasets.make_circles(n_samples=n_samples, factor=.5, noise=.05)[0]
plt.scatter(data[:,0], data[:,1])
plt.show()
```

The first line imports the utility from the scikit-learn library. Next, the number of instances is set to **1500**. A variable named **data** is created to store the values, which are created by using the **make_circles()** function. Finally, a scatter plot is drawn to display the data points in a data space, which looks similar to the one shown here.

> **Note**
>
> The Matplotlib function **show()** is used to trigger the display of the plot, considering that the above lines only create it. When programming in Jupyter Notebooks it is not required, but in any other environment is required.

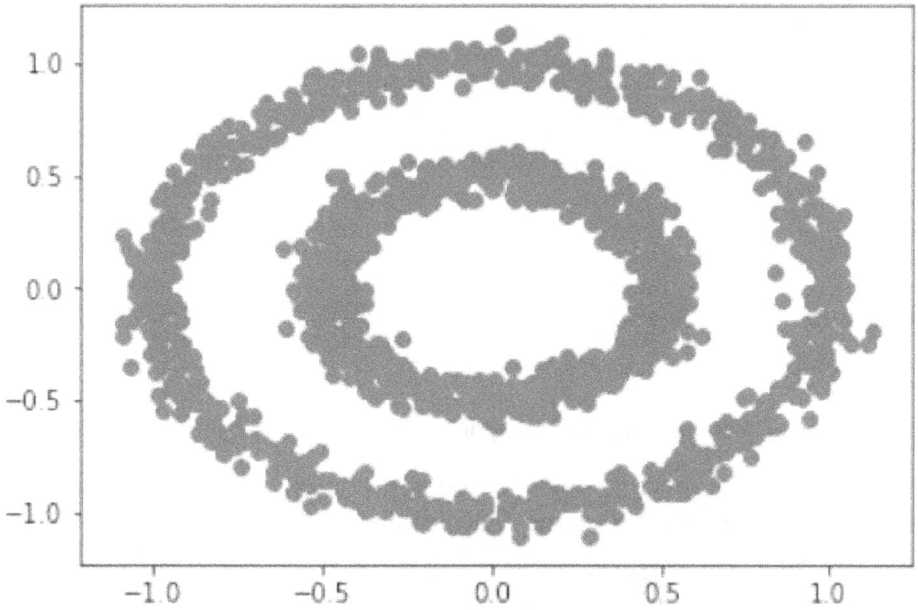

Figure 2.4: A scatter plot of the noisy circles dataset

The final output is a dataset with two features and 1,500 instances.

> **Note**
>
> The **make_circles()** function is used to create a toy dataset to visualize clustering algorithms. It works by making a large circle containing a smaller circle in 2D.
> To learn more about the **make_circles()** function, visit the documentation of scikit-learn in the following link: http://scikit-learn.org/stable/modules/generated/sklearn.datasets.make_circles.html.

4. Create a histogram out of one of the two features:

```
plt.hist(data[:,0])
plt.show()
```

The plot will look similar to the one shown below:

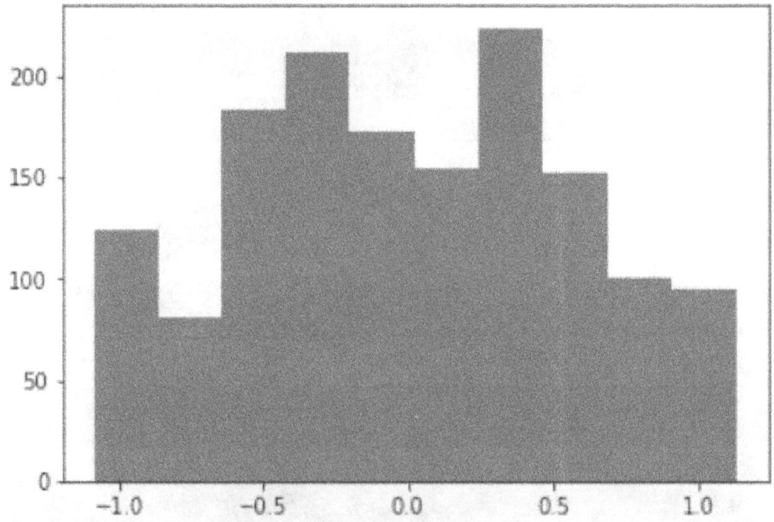

Figure 2.5: A screenshot showing the histogram obtained using data from the first feature

Congratulations! You have successfully created a histogram using Matplotlib. Similarly, different plot types can be created using Matplotlib.

In conclusion, visualization tools help you better understand the data available in a dataset, the results from a model, and the performance of the model. This happens because the human brain is receptive to visual forms, instead of large files of data.

Matplotlib has become one of the most commonly used libraries to perform data visualization. Among the different plot types that the library supports are histograms bar charts, and scatter plots.

Activity 3: Using Data Visualization to Aid the Preprocessing Process

Before you proceed with this section, follow these steps to download the dataset that you will use for this activity:

1. Access the following link: http://archive.ics.uci.edu/ml/datasets/Wholesale+customers.
2. Below the dataset's title, find the download section and click on **Data Folder**.
3. Click on **Wholesale customers data.csv** to trigger the download and save the file in the same path as that of your current Jupyter Notebook.

The marketing team of your company wants to know the different profiles of its clients to focus its marketing effort to suit the individual needs of each profile. To do so, it has provided your team with a list of 440 pieces of previous sales data. Your first task is to preprocess the data, and your boss has asked you to specifically use data visualization to help him understand the decisions you took in that process. For this purpose, you need to load a CSV dataset using Pandas and use data visualization tools to help the preprocessing process. The following steps will guide you:

1. Load the previously downloaded dataset by using the Pandas function `read_csv()`, given that the dataset is stored in a CSV file. Store the dataset in a Pandas DataFrame named `data`.

> **Note**
>
> Make sure to import the required libraries first. For instance, Pandas and Matplotlib.

2. Check for missing values in your DataFrame. If present, handle the missing values and support your decision with data visualization.

> **Note**
>
> Use `data.isnull().sum()` to check the entire dataset at once.

3. Check for outliers in your DataFrame. If present, handle the outliers and support your decision with data visualization.

> **Note**
>
> Mark as outliers all the values that are three standard deviations away from the mean.

4. Rescale the data using the formula for normalization or standardization.

> **Note**
>
> Standardization tends to work better for clustering purposes. Also, you can find the solution for this activity on page 185.

On checking the above, you should find no missing values in the dataset and 6 features with outliers that are to be handled.

k-means Algorithm

The k-means algorithm is used for data without a labeled class. It involves dividing the data into K number of subgroups. The classification of data points into each group is done based on similarity, as explained before, which for this algorithm is measured by the distance from the center (centroid) of the cluster. The final output of the algorithm are the data points related to a cluster and the centroid of each cluster, which can be used to label new data in the same clusters.

The centroid of each cluster represents a collection of features that can be used to define the nature of the data points that belong there.

Understanding the Algorithm

The k-means algorithm works through an iterative process that involves the following steps:

1. Based on the number of clusters defined by the user, the centroids are generated either by setting initial estimates or by randomly choosing them from the data points. This step is known as *initialization*.

2. All the data points are assigned to the nearest cluster in the data space by measuring their respective distances from the centroid, known as the *assignment step*. The objective is to minimize the squared Euclidean distance, which can be defined by the following formula:

$$\min dist(c, x)^2$$

Figure 2.6: A formula minimizing the Euclidean distance

Here, *c* represents a centroid, *x* refers to a data point, and *dist()* is the Euclidean distance.

3. Centroids are calculated again by computing the mean of all data points belonging to a cluster. This step is known as the *update step*.

Steps 2 and 3 are repeated in an iterative process, until a criterion is met. The criterion can be as follows:

- The number of iterations defined.
- The data points do not change from cluster to cluster.
- The Euclidean distance is minimized.

The algorithm is set to always arrive at a result, even though this result may converge to a local or a global optimum.

The k-means algorithm receives several parameters as inputs to run the model. The most important ones to consider are the initialization methods (`init`) and the number of clusters (**K**), which are explained as follows.

> **Note**
>
> To check out the other parameters of the k-means algorithm in the scikit-learn library, visit the following link: http://scikit-learn.org/stable/modules/generated/sklearn.cluster.KMeans.html.

Initialization Methods

An important input of the algorithm is the initialization method to be used to generate the initial centroids. The initialization methods allowed by the scikit-learn library are explained as follows:

1. **k-means++**: This is the default option. Centroids are chosen randomly from the set of data points, considering that centroids must be far away from one another. To achieve this, the method assigns a higher probability of being a centroid to those data points that are farther away from other centroids.
2. **random**: This method chooses K observations randomly from the data points as the initial centroids.

Choosing the Number of Clusters

As discussed previously, the number of clusters into which the data is to be divided is set by the user; hence, it is important to choose the number of clusters appropriately.

One of the metrics used to measure the performance of the k-means algorithm is the mean distance of the data points from the centroid of the cluster that they belong to. However, this measure can be counterproductive as the higher the number of clusters, the smaller the distance between the data points and its centroid, which may result in the number of clusters (K) matching the number of data points, thereby harming the purpose of clustering algorithms.

To avoid this, an approach that can be followed is to plot the average distance between data points and its center against the number of clusters. The appropriate number of clusters corresponds to the breaking point of the plot, where the rate of decrease drastically changes. In the following diagram, the dotted circle represents the ideal number of clusters:

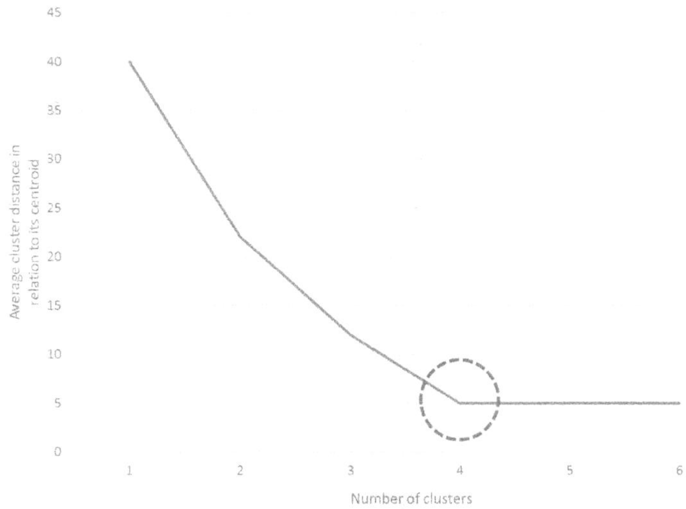

Figure 2.7: A graph demonstrating how to estimate the breaking point

Exercise 6: Importing and Training the k-means Algorithm over a Dataset

The following exercise will be performed using the same dataset that was created in the previous exercise using the **make_circles()** function. Considering this, use the same Jupyter Notebook that you used to develop the previous exercise:

1. Open the Jupyter Notebook that you used for the previous exercise. Here, you should have imported all the required libraries and stored the dataset in a variable named **data**.
2. Import the k-means algorithm from scikit-learn, by using the following code:

```
from sklearn.cluster import KMeans
```

3. To choose the value for K, calculate the average distance of data points from its centroid in relation to the number of clusters. Consider that the maximum numbers of clusters to be created should not exceed 20. The following is a snippet of the code:

```
ideal_k = []
for i in range(1,21):
  est_kmeans = KMeans(n_clusters=i)
  est_kmeans.fit(data)

  ideal_k.append([i,est_kmeans.inertia_])
```

First, create the variables that will store the values as an array and name it **ideal_k**. Next, perform a **for** loop that starts at one cluster and goes as high as desired (considering that the max number of clusters must not exceed the number of instances).

For the previous example, there was a limitation of maximum 20 clusters to be created. As a consequence to this limitation, the **for** loop goes from 1 to 20 clusters.

> **Note**
>
> Remember that **range()** is an upper bound exclusive function, meaning that the range will go as far as one value below the upper bound. When the upper bound is 21, the range will go as far as 20.

Inside the **for** loop, initialize the algorithm with the number of clusters to be created, and then fit the data to the model. Next, append the pairs of data (number of clusters, average distance to the centroid) to the list named **ideal_k**:

```
ideal_k = np.array(ideal_k)
```

The average distance to the centroid does not need to be calculated as the model outputs it under the attribute **inertia_**, which can be called out as **[model_name].inertia_**.

Finally, the **ideal_k** list is converted into a NumPy array so that you are able to feed it as a parameter of a Matplotlib plot.

4. Plot the relations calculated in the preceding step to find the ideal K to input to the final model:

```
plt.plot(ideal_k[:,0],ideal_k[:,1])
plt.show()
```

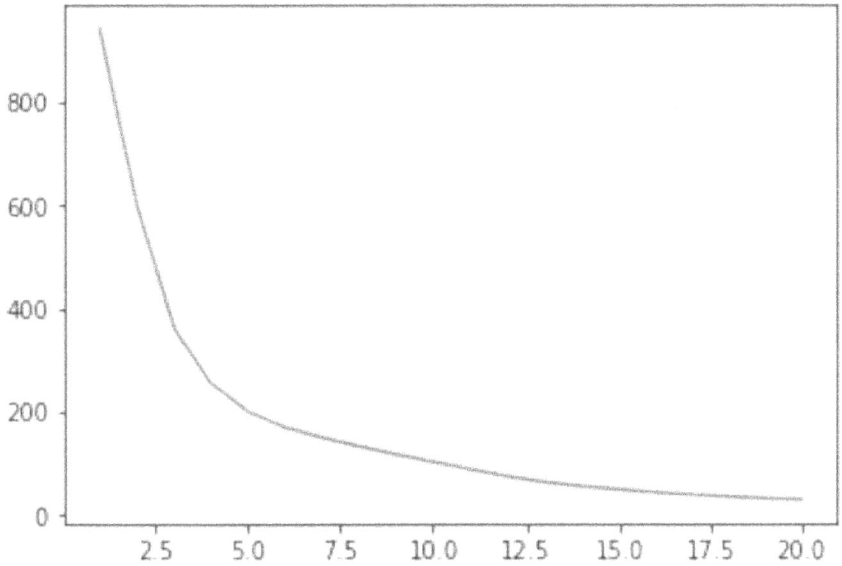

Figure 2.8: A screenshot showing the output of the plot function used

The breaking point of the plot is around 5.

5. Train the model with **K=5**. Use the following code:

```
est_kmeans = KMeans(n_clusters=5)
est_kmeans.fit(data)
pred_kmeans = est_kmeans.predict(data)
```

The first line initializes the model with 5 as the number of clusters. Then, the data is fit to the model. Finally, the model is used to assign a cluster to each data point.

6. Plot the results from the clustering of data points into clusters:

```
plt.scatter(data[:,0], data[:,1], c=pred_kmeans)
plt.show()
```

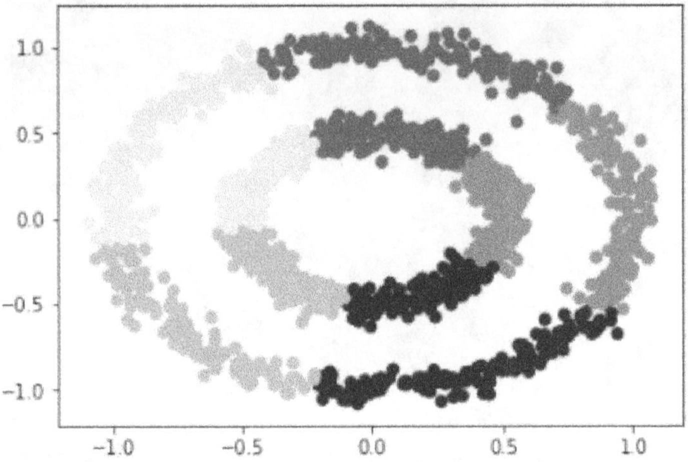

Figure 2.9: A screenshot showing the output of the plot function used

Since the dataset only contains two features, each feature is passed as input to the scatter plot function. Additionally, the labels obtained from the clustering process are used as the colors to display the data points. Thus, each data point is located in the data space based on the values of both features, and the colors represent the clusters that were formed.

> **Note**
>
> For datasets with over two features, the visual representation of clusters is not as explicit as the shown in the preceding screenshot. This is mainly because the location of each data point (observation) in the data space is based on the collection of all of its features, and visually it is only possible to display up to three features.

Congratulations! You have successfully imported and trained the k-means algorithm.

In conclusion, the k-means algorithm seeks to divide the data into K number of clusters, K being a parameter set by the user. Data points are grouped together based on their proximity to the centroid of a cluster, which is calculated by an iterative process.

The initial centroids are set according to the initialization method defined. Then, all data points are assigned to the clusters with the centroid closer to their location in the data space, using the Euclidean distance as measure. Once the data points are divided into clusters, the centroid of each cluster is recalculated as the mean of all data points. The process is repeated several times until a stopping criterion is met.

Activity 4: Applying the k-means Algorithm to a Dataset

Ensure that you have completed Activity 3 before you proceed with this activity.

Continuing with the analysis of your company's past orders, you are now in charge of applying the k-means algorithm over the dataset. Using the previously loaded Wholesale Customers dataset, apply the k-means algorithm to the data and classify the data into clusters. Follow these steps to complete this activity:

1. Open the Jupyter Notebook that you used for the previous activity. There, you should have imported all the required libraries and stored the dataset in a variable named `data`.
2. Calculate the average distance of the data points from its centroid in relation to the number of clusters. Based on this distance, select the appropriate number of clusters to train the model.
3. Train the model and assign a cluster to each data point in your dataset. Plot the results.

> **Note**
>
> You can use the **`subplots()`** function from Matplotlib to plot two scatter graphs at a time. To learn more about this function, visit Matplotlib's documentation at the following link: https://matplotlib.org/api/_as_gen/matplotlib.pyplot.subplots.html.
> Also, you can find the solution for this activity on page 189.

The visualization of clusters will differ based on the number of clusters (k) and the features selected to be plotted.

Mean-Shift Algorithm

The **mean-shift algorithm** works by assigning each data point a cluster based on the density of data points in the data space, also known as the mode in a distribution function. Contrary to the k-means algorithm, the mean-shift algorithm does not require you to specify the number of clusters as a parameter.

The algorithm works by modeling the data points as a distribution function, where high-density areas (high concentration of data points) represent high peaks. Then, the general idea is to shift each data point until it reaches its nearest peak, which becomes a cluster.

Understanding the Algorithm

The first step of the mean-shift algorithm is the representation of the data points as a density distribution. To do so, the algorithm builds upon the idea of **Kernel Density Estimation** (**KDE**), which is a method used to estimate the distribution of a set of data:

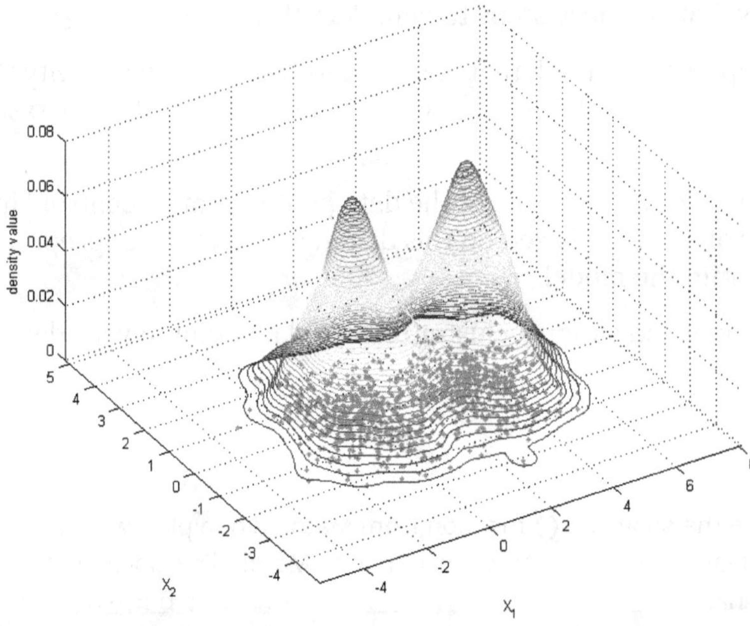

Figure 2.10: An image depicting the idea behind Kernel Density Estimation

In the preceding diagram, the red dots represent the data points that the user inputs and the colored lines represent the estimated distribution of the data points. The peaks (high-density areas) will be the clusters. The process of assigning data points to each cluster is explained next:

1. A window of a specified size (bandwidth) is drawn around each data point.
2. The mean of the data inside the window is computed.
3. The center of the window is shifted to the mean.

Steps 2 and 3 are repeated until the data point reaches a peak, which will determine the cluster to which it belongs.

The bandwidth value should be coherent with the distribution of the data points in the dataset. For example, for a dataset normalized between 0 and 1, the bandwidth value should be within that range, while for a dataset with all values between 1.000 and 2.000, it would make more sense to have a bandwidth between 100 and 500.

In the following diagram, the estimated distribution is represented by the lines, and the data points are the red dots. In each of the boxes, the data points shift to the nearest peak. All the data points in a certain peak belong to that cluster:

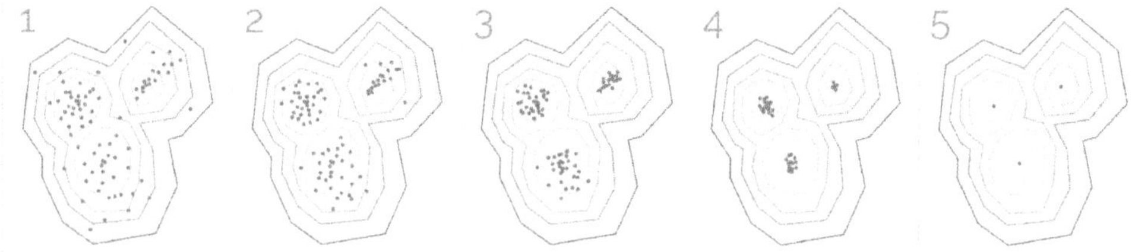

Figure 2.11: A sequence of images illustrating the working of the mean-shift algorithm

The number of shifts that a data point has to make to reach a peak depends on its bandwidth (the size of the window) and its distance from the peak.

> **Note**
>
> To explore all the parameters of the mean-shift algorithm in scikit-learn, visit http://scikit-learn.org/stable/modules/generated/sklearn.cluster.MeanShift.html.

Exercise 7: Importing and Training the Mean-Shift Algorithm over a Dataset

The following exercise will be performed using the same dataset that was created in the first exercise of this chapter. Considering this, use the same Jupyter Notebook that you used to develop the previous exercise:

1. Open the Jupyter Notebook that you used for the previous exercise.
2. Import the k-means algorithm class from scikit-learn by using the following code:

```
from sklearn.cluster import MeanShift
```

3. Train the model with a bandwidth of 0.5:

```
est_meanshift = MeanShift(0.5)
est_meanshift.fit(data)
pred_meanshift = est_meanshift.predict(data)
```

Considering that the dataset has created values ranging from –1 to 1, the bandwidth value should not be above 1. The value of 0.5 was chosen after trying out other values, such as 0.1 and 0.9.

> **Note**
>
> Take into account that the bandwidth is a parameter of the algorithm, and as a parameter, it can be fine-tuned to arrive at the best performance. The fine-tuning process will be further evaluated in later chapters.

First, the model is initialized with a bandwidth of 0.5. Next, the model is fit to the data. Finally, the model is used to assign a cluster to each data point.

4. Plot the results from the clustering of data points into clusters:

```
plt.scatter(data[:,0], data[:,1], c=pred_meanshift)
plt.show()
```

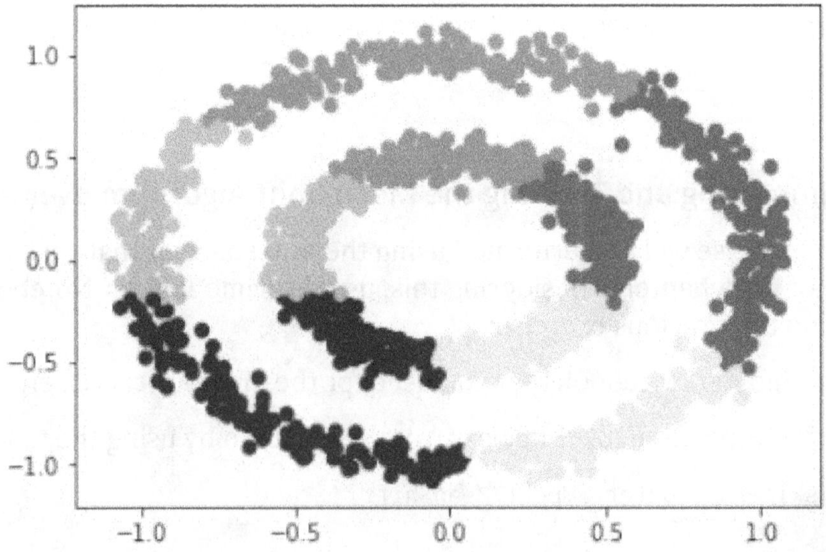

Figure 2.12: The plot obtained using the preceding code

Again, as the dataset only contains two features, both are passed as inputs to the scatter function. Also, the labels obtained from the clustering process are used as the colors to display the data points.

The total number of clusters that has been created is four.

Congratulations! You have successfully imported and trained the mean-shift algorithm.

In conclusion, the mean-shift algorithm starts by drawing the distribution function that represents the set of data points. This process consists of creating peaks in high-density areas, while leaving flat the areas with a low density.

Following this, the algorithm proceeds to classify the data points into clusters by shifting each point slowly and iteratively until it reaches a peak, which becomes its cluster.

Activity 5: Applying the Mean-Shift Algorithm to a Dataset

Your boss wants you to also apply the mean-shift algorithm to the dataset to see which algorithm fits the data better. Therefore, using the previously loaded Wholesale Consumers dataset, apply the mean-shift algorithm to the data and classify the data into clusters. Follow these steps to complete this activity:

1. Open the Jupyter Notebook that you used for the previous activity.

> **Note**
>
> Considering that you are using the same Jupyter Notebook, be careful not to overwrite a previous variable.

2. Train the model and assign a cluster to each data point in your dataset. Plot the results.

> **Note**
>
> The solution for this activity can be found on page 192.

The visualization of clusters will differ based on the bandwidth and the features selected to be plotted.

DBSCAN Algorithm

The **density-based spatial clustering of applications with noise** (**DBSCAN**) algorithm groups together points that are close to each other (with many neighbors) and marks those points that are further away with no close neighbors as outliers.

According to this, and as its name states, the algorithm classifies data points based on the density of all data points in the data space.

Understanding the Algorithm

The DBSCAN algorithm requires two main parameters: epsilon and the minimum number of observations.

Epsilon, also known as `eps`, is the maximum distance that defines the radius within which the algorithm searches for neighbors. The **minimum number of observations**, on the other hand, refers to the number of data points required to form a high density area (`min_samples`). However, the latter is optional in scikit-learn as the default value is set to 5:

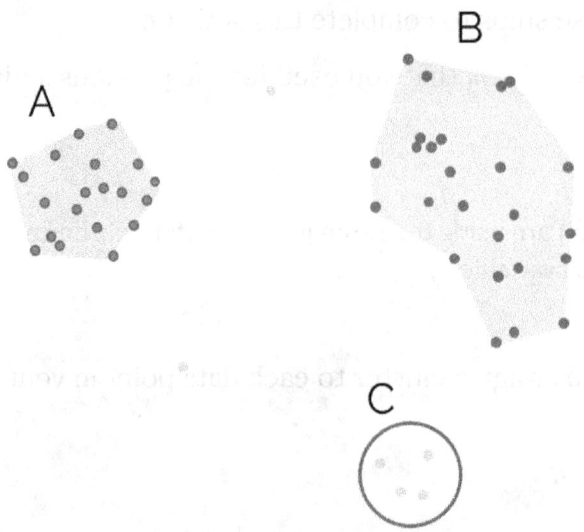

Figure 2.13: An illustration of how the DBSCAN algorithm classifies data into clusters

In the preceding diagram, the blue dots are assigned to the blue shaded cluster (A) and the orange dots are assigned to the orange shaded cluster (B). Moreover, the yellow dots (C) are considered to be outliers, as they do not meet the required parameters to belong to a high-density area.

Some areas with a small concentration of points, such as the yellow dots at the bottom of the image (C), may not constitute a cluster as the minimum number of data points to form a high-density area is not met (which, for this example, is set to 5).

> **Note**
>
> Similar to the bandwidth parameter, the epsilon value should be coherent with the distribution of the data points in the dataset considering that it represents a radius around each data point.

According to this, each data point can be classified as follows:

- **A core point**: A point that has at least the minimum number of data points within its **eps** radius.
- **A border point**: A point that is within the *eps* radius of a core point, but does not have the required number of data points within its own radius.
- **A noise point**: All point that do not meet the preceding descriptions.

> **Note**
>
> To explore all parameters of the DBSCAN algorithm in scikit-learn, visit http://scikit-learn.org/stable/modules/generated/sklearn.cluster.DBSCAN.html.

Exercise 8: Importing and Training the DBSCAN Algorithm over a Dataset

This exercise discusses how to import and train the DBSCAN algorithm over a dataset. We will be using the dataset that we created in the first exercise of this chapter for this activity:

1. Open the Jupyter Notebook that you used for the previous exercise.
2. Import the DBSCAN algorithm class from scikit-learn by using the following code:

   ```
   from sklearn.cluster import DBSCAN
   ```

3. Train the model with **epsilon** equal to 0.1:

   ```
   est_dbscan = DBSCAN(eps=0.1)
   pred_dbscan = est_dbscan.fit_predict(data)
   ```

   First, the model is initialized with **eps** of 0.1. Then, we use the **fit_predict()** function to both fit the model to the data and assign a cluster to each data point.

This bundled function, which includes both the **fit** and **predict** method at once, is used because the DBSCAN algorithm in scikit-learn does not contain a **predict()** method alone.

Again, the value of 0.1 was chosen after trying out other possible values.

4. Plot the results from the clustering process:

```
plt.scatter(data[:,0], data[:,1], c=pred_dbscan)
plt.show()
```

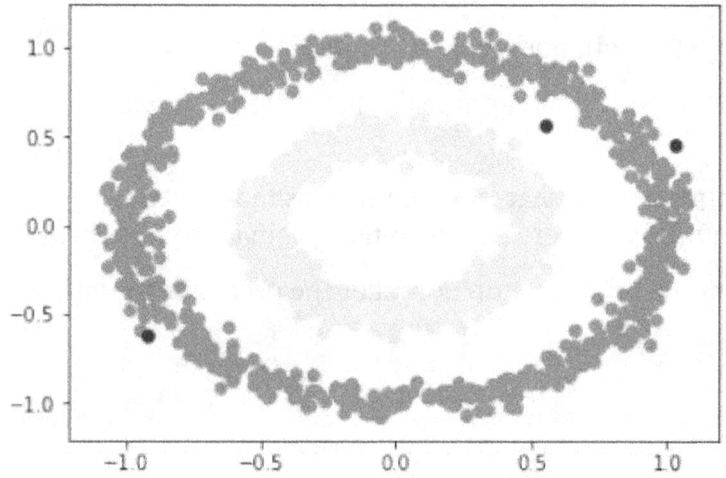

Figure 2.14: The plot obtained with the preceding code

As before, both features are passed as inputs to the scatter function. Also, the labels obtained from the clustering process are used as the colors to display the data points.

The total number of clusters that have been created is two.

As you can see, the total number of clusters created by each algorithm is different. This is because, as mentioned previously, each of these algorithms defines similarity differently, and as a consequence, each one of them interprets the data differently.

Due to this, it is crucial to test different algorithms over the data to compare the results and define which one generalizes better to the data. The following topic will explore some methods to evaluate performance to help choose an algorithm.

Congratulations! You have successfully imported and trained the DBSCAN algorithm.

In conclusion, the DBSCAN algorithm bases its clustering classification on the density of data points in the data space. This means that clusters are formed by data points with many neighbors. This is done by considering that core points are those that contain a minimum number of neighbors within a set radius, border points are those that are located inside the radius of a core point but do not have the minimum number of neighbors within their own radius, and noise points are those that do not meet any of the specifications.

Activity 6: Applying the DBSCAN Algorithm to the Dataset

Thanks to your excellent work and fast turnaround, your boss wants you to also apply the DBSCAN algorithm to the dataset. Using the previously loaded Wholesale Consumers dataset, apply the DBSCAN algorithm to the data and classify the data into clusters. Follow the following steps:

1. Open the Jupyter Notebook that you used for the previous activity.
2. Train the model and assign a cluster to each data point in your dataset. Plot the results.

> **Note**
>
> The solution for this activity can be found on page 193.

The visualization of clusters will differ based on the epsilon and the features selected to be plotted.

Evaluating the Performance of Clusters

After applying a clustering algorithm, it is necessary to evaluate how well the algorithm has performed. This is especially important when it is difficult to visually evaluate the clusters, for example, when there are several features.

Usually, with **supervised algorithms**, it is easy to evaluate the performance by simply comparing the prediction of each instance with its true value (class). On the other hand, when dealing with **unsupervised models**, it is necessary to pursue other strategies. In the specific case of clustering algorithms, it is possible to evaluate performance by measuring the similarity of the data points that belong to the same cluster.

Available Metrics in Scikit-Learn

Scikit-learn allows its users to use two different scores for evaluating the performance of unsupervised clustering algorithms. The main idea behind these scores is to measure how well-defined the cluster's edges are, instead of measuring the dispersion within a cluster. Hence, it is worth mentioning that the scores do not take into account the size of each cluster.

The **Silhouette Coefficient Score** calculates the mean distance between each point and all the other points of a cluster (*a*), as well as the mean distance between each point and all the other points of its nearest clusters (*b*). It relates both of them according to the following equation:

$$s = (b - a)/\max(a, b)$$

Figure 2.15: An equation showing how the silhouette coefficient score is calculated

The result of the score is a value between -1 and 1. The lower the value, the worse the performance of the algorithm. Values around 0 will imply overlapping of clusters. It is also important to clarify that this score does not work very well when using density-based algorithms such as DBSCAN.

The **Calinski–Harabasz Index** was created to measure the relation between the variance of each cluster and the variance of all clusters. More specifically, the variance of each cluster is the mean square error of each point with respect to the centroid of that cluster. On the other hand, the variance of all clusters refers to the overall inter-cluster variance.

The higher the value of the Calinski–Harabasz Index, the better the definition and separation of the clusters. There is no acceptable cut-off value, so the performance of the algorithms using this index is evaluated through comparison, where the algorithm with the highest value is the one that performs best. As with the Silhouette Coefficient, this score does not perform well on density-based algorithms such as DBSCAN.

Unfortunately, the scikit-learn library does not contain other methods for effectively measuring the performance of density-based clustering algorithms, and although the methods mentioned here may work in some cases to measure the performance of these algorithms, when they do not, there is no other way to measure this other than via manual evaluation.

Exercise 9: Evaluating the Silhouette Coefficient Score and Calinski–Harabasz Index

In this exercise, we will learn how to estimate the two scores discussed in the previous section in scikit-learn:

1. Import the Silhouette Coefficient score from the scikit-learn library:

   ```
   from sklearn.metrics import silhouette_score
   ```

2. Calculate the Silhouette Coefficient score for each of the algorithms created in all of the previous exercises. Use the Euclidean distance as the metric for measuring the distance between points.

   The input parameters of the **`silhouette_score()`** function are the data, the predicted values of the model (the clusters assigned to each data point), and the distance measure:

   ```
   kmeans_score = silhouette_score(data, pred_kmeans, metric='euclidean')
   meanshift_score = silhouette_score(data, pred_meanshift,
   metric='euclidean')
   dbscan_score = silhouette_score(data, pred_dbscan, metric='euclidean')
   print(kmeans_score, meanshift_score, dbscan_score)
   ```

   The scores come to be around 0.359, 0.344, and 0.0893 for the k-means, mean-shift, and DBSCAN algorithms, respectively.

   You can observe that both k-means and mean-shift algorithms have similar scores, while the DBSCAN score is closer to zero. This can indicate that the performance of the first two algorithms is much better, and hence, the DBSCAN algorithm should not be considered to solve the data problem.

   Nevertheless, it is important to remember that this type of score does not perform well when evaluating the DBSCAN algorithm. This is basically because as one cluster is surrounding the other one, the score can interpret that as an overlap when in reality the clusters are very well-defined.

3. Import the Calinski-Harabasz Index from the scikit-learn library:

   ```
   from sklearn.metrics import calinski_harabaz_score
   ```

4. Calculate the Calinski-Harabasz index for each of the algorithms created in the previous exercises in this chapter. The input parameters of the **calinski_harabaz_score()** function are the data and the predicted values of the model (the clusters assigned to each data point):

```
kmeans_score = calinski_harabaz_score(data, pred_kmeans)
meanshift_score = calinski_harabaz_score(data, pred_meanshift)
dbscan_score = calinski_harabaz_score(data, pred_dbscan)
print(kmeans_score, meanshift_score, dbscan_score)
```

   The values come to approximately 1377.8, 1304.07, and 0.158 for the k-means, mean-shift, and DBSCAN algorithms, respectively. Once again, the results are similar to the ones obtained using the Silhouette Coefficient score, where both the k-means and mean-shift algorithms performed similarly well, while the DBSCAN algorithm did not.

   Moreover, it is worth mentioning that the scale of each method (the Silhouette Coefficient score and the Calinski-Harabasz index) differs significantly, so they are not easily comparable.

Congratulations! You have successfully measured the performance of three different clustering algorithms.

In conclusion, the scores presented in this topic are a way of evaluating the performance of clustering algorithms. However, it is important to consider that the results from these scores are not definitive as their performance varies from algorithm to algorithm.

Activity 7: Measuring and Comparing the Performance of the Algorithms

Your boss is not sure about the performance of the algorithms as it cannot be evaluated graphically. Therefore, she has asked you to measure the performance of the algorithms using numerical metrics that she can use to make comparisons. You need to use the previously trained models and calculate the Silhouette Coefficient score and the Calinski-Harabasz index to measure the performance of the algorithms. The following steps provide hints regarding how you can do this:

1. Open the Jupyter Notebook that you used for the previous activity.

2. Calculate both the Silhouette Coefficient score and the Calinski-Harabasz index for all of the models that you trained previously.

> **Note**
>
> The solution for this activity can be found on page 195.

The results may differ based on the choices made during the activities and the initialization of certain parameters in each algorithm.

Summary

Data problems where the input data is unrelated to a labeled output is handled using unsupervised learning. The main objective of such data problems is to understand the data by finding patterns that, in some cases, can be generalized to new instances. In this context, this chapter covered clustering algorithms, which work by aggregating similar data points into clusters, while separating data points that greatly differ. After this, the chapter covered data visualization tools that can be used to analyze problematic features during data preprocessing. We also saw how to apply different algorithms to the dataset and compare their performance to choose the one that best fits the data. Two different metrics for performance evaluation, the Silhouette Coefficient metric and the Calinski-Harabasz index, were also discussed in light of the inability to represent all of the features in a plot, and thereby graphically evaluate performance on scikit-learn. However, it is important to understand that the result from the metric performance is not absolute, as some metrics perform better (by default) for some algorithms than for others.

In the next chapter, we will understand the steps involved in working with a supervised machine learning algorithm, and learn how to perform error analysis.

3

Supervised Learning: Key Steps

Learning Objectives

By the end of this chapter, you will be able to:

- Explain the difference between training, validation, and testing sets
- Perform data partitioning for split or cross validation
- Describe the different metrics to evaluate performance
- Choose the performance metric that fits the purpose of the study
- Perform error analysis

This chapter explains the methodology to approach a machine learning classification problem.

Introduction

In the previous chapter, we saw how to solve data problems using unsupervised learning algorithms and applied the concepts that we learned to some real-life datasets. We also learned how to compare the performance of various algorithms and studied two different metrics for performance evaluation.

In this chapter, we will explore the main steps for working on a supervised machine learning problem. First, the chapter explains the different sets in which data needs to be split for training, validating, and testing your model. Next, the most common evaluation metrics will be explained. It is important to highlight that, among all the metrics available, only one should be selected as the evaluation metric of the study, and its selection should be made by considering the purpose of the study. Finally, the students will learn how to perform error analysis, with the purpose of understanding what measures to take to improve the results of a model.

Model Validation and Testing

Nowadays, it is easy for almost anybody to start working in a machine-learning project with all the information available online. However, choosing the right algorithm for your data is a challenge when there are many alternatives available. Due to this, the right algorithm is chosen by a process of trial and error, where the different alternatives are tested.

Moreover, the decision process to arrive at a good model covers not only the selection of the algorithm but also the tuning of its hyperparameters. To do this, a conventional approach is to divide the data into three parts, training, validation, and testing sets, which will be explained further now.

Data Partition

Data partition is a process involving the division of the dataset into three subsets so that each set can be used for a different purpose. This way, the development of a model is not affected by the introduction of bias. The following is an explanation of each subset:

- **Training set**: As the name suggests, this is the portion of the dataset used for training the model. It consists of the input data (the observations) paired with an outcome (the label class).

  This set can be used to train as many models as desired, using different algorithms. However, performance evaluation is not done over this set.

- **Validation set**: Also known as the **dev set**, this set is used to perform an unbiased evaluation of each model while fine-tuning the hyperparameters. Performance evaluation is frequently done over this set of data to test different configurations of the hyperparameters.

  Although the model does not learn from this data, but from the training set data, it is indirectly affected by the data in this set due to its participation in the process of deciding the changes over the parameters.

  After running different configurations of hyperparameters and based on the performance of the model over the validation set, a winning model is selected for each algorithm.

- **Testing set**: This is used to perform the final evaluation of performance of the model (after training and validation) over unseen data. This helps measure the performance of the model with real-life data for future predictions.

  The testing set is also used to compare competing models. Considering that the training set was used to train different models and the validation set was used to fine-tune the hyperparameters of each model to select a winning configuration, the purpose of the testing set is to perform an unbiased comparison of the final models.

The diagram below shows the process of selecting the ideal model and using the sets mentioned previously.

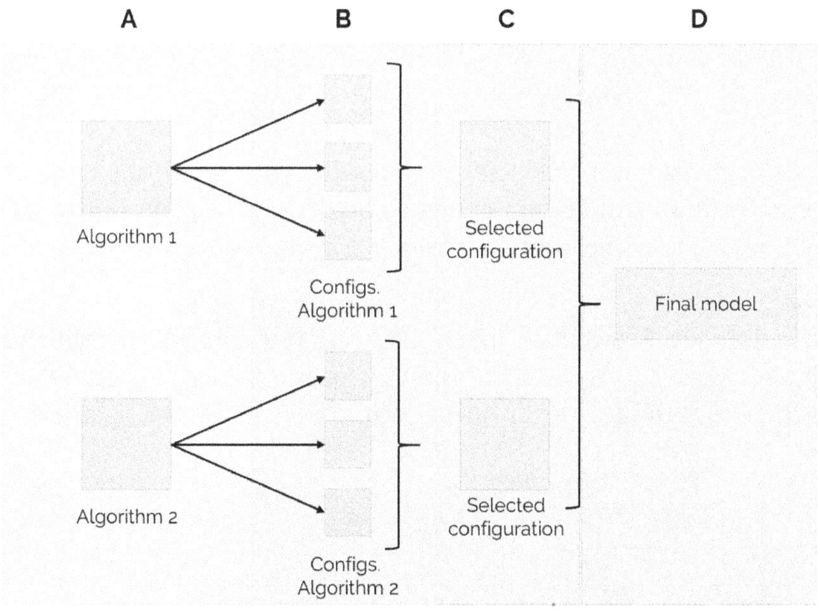

Figure 3.1: Dataset partition purposes

The sections A–D shown in the preceding figure previously are described below:

- Section A refers to the process of training the model for the desired algorithms, using the data contained in the training set.
- Section B represents the fine-tuning process of the hyperparameters of each model. The selection of the best configuration of hyperparameters is based on the performance of the model over the validation set.
- Section C shows the process of selecting the final model by comparing the final configuration of each algorithm based on their performance over the testing set.
- Finally, section D represents the selected model that will be applied to real-life data for prediction.

Initially, machine learning problems were solved by only partitioning data into two sets: a training and a testing set. This approach consisted of using the training set to train the model, which is the same as the approach with three sets. However, the testing set was used for fine-tuning the hyperparameters as well as for determining the ultimate performance of the algorithm.

Although this approach can also work, models that are created using this approach do not always perform equally well over unseen real-life data. This is mainly because, as mentioned previously, the use of the set to fine-tune the hyperparameters indirectly introduces bias to the model.

Considering this, there is one way to achieve a less biased model while dividing the dataset into two sets, which is called a **cross-validation split**. We will explore this later.

Split Ratio

Now that the differences among the purposes of the various sets is clear, it is important to clarify the split ratio in which data needs to be divided. Although there is no exact science for calculating the split radio, there are a couple of things to consider when doing so:

- **Size of the dataset**: Previously, when data was not easily available, datasets contained between 100 to 100,000 instances, and the conventionally accepted split ratio was 60/20/20% for the training, validation, and testing sets, respectively.

Nowadays, with software and hardware improving every day, researchers can put together datasets that contain over a million instances. This capacity to gather huge amounts of data allows the split ratio to be 98/1/1%, respectively. This is mainly because the larger the dataset, the more data that can be used for training a model, without compromising the amount of data left for the validation and testing sets.

- **The algorithm**: It is important to consider that some algorithms may require higher amounts of data to train a model. In this case, like with the preceding approaches, you should always opt for a larger training set.

  Other algorithms, for example, do not require the validation and testing sets to be split equally. For instance, a model with fewer hyperparameters can be easily tuned, which allows the validation set to be smaller than the testing set. However, if a model has many hyperparameters, you will need to have a larger validation set.

Nevertheless, even though the preceding measures serve as a guide for splitting the dataset, it is always important to consider the distribution of your dataset and the purpose of the study. Considering that the model is going to be used with data with a different distribution than the one used to train the model, the real-life data, even if limited, must at least be a part of the testing set to make sure that the model will work for the desired purpose.

The following diagram displays the proportional partition of the dataset into three subsets. It is important to highlight that the training set must be larger than the other two, as it is the one to be used for training the model. Additionally, it is possible to observe that both the training and validation sets have an effect on the model, while the testing set is mainly used to validate the actual performance of the model with real-life data. Considering this, the training and validation sets must come from the same distribution:

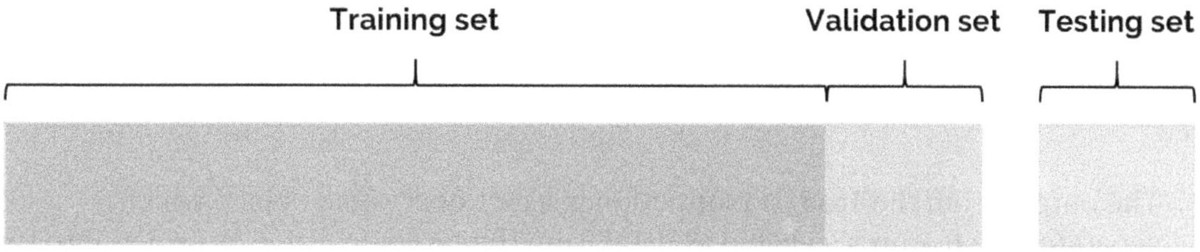

Figure 3.2: Visualization of the split ratio

Exercise 10: Performing Data Partition over a Sample Dataset

In this exercise, we will be performing data partition over the **iris** dataset using the split ratio method.

> **Note**
>
> For the exercises and activities within this chapter, you will need to have Python 3.6, NumPy, Jupyter, Pandas, and scikit-learn installed on your system.

1. Open a Jupyter Notebook to implement this exercise. The partition in this exercise will be done using the three-splits approach.
2. Import the **iris** toy dataset using scikit-learn's datasets package and store it in a variable named **iris_data**. Use the following code snippet:

```
from sklearn.datasets import load_iris
iris_data = load_iris()
```

> **Note**
>
> It is a good practice to import all of the required libraries, packages, and modules at the beginning of your project. However, during the following exercises and activities, it will not be handled this way for visualization purposes.

The first line imports the **load_iris** function from scikit-learn's datasets package. This function loads a toy dataset provided by scikit-learn. Next, we execute the method to retrieve the output.

> **Note**
>
> To check the characteristics of the dataset, visit the following link: http://scikit-learn.org/stable/modules/generated/sklearn.datasets.load_iris.html.

The output from the **load_iris** function is a dictionary-like object, which separates the features (callable as data) from the target (callable as target) into two attributes.

3. Convert each attribute (data and target) into a Pandas DataFrame to facilitate data manipulation. To do this, first import Pandas, and then create both DataFrames. Print the shape of both DataFrames:

```
import pandas as pd
X = pd.DataFrame(iris_data.data)
Y = pd.DataFrame(iris_data.target)
print(X.shape, Y.shape)
```

The output from the print function should be as follows:

```
(150,4) (150,1)
```

Here, the values in the first parenthesis represent the shape of the DataFrame **X** (known as the features matrix) and the values in the second parenthesis refer to the shape of the DataFrame **Y** (known as the target matrix).

> **Note**
>
> The scikit-learn library has a function to partition data into two subsets (a train and a test set). As the objective of this exercise is to partition data into three subsets, the function will be used twice to achieve the desired result.

4. Import the **train_test_split** function from scikit-learn's **model_selection** package:

```
from sklearn.model_selection import train_test_split
```

5. Perform a first split of the data using the function that we just imported. Use the following code snippet:

```
X_train, X_test, Y_train, Y_test = train_test_split(X, Y, test_size = 0.2)
```

The inputs of the **train_test_split** function are the two matrices **(X,Y)** and the size of the test set, as a value between 0 and 1, that represents the proportion.

> **Note**
>
> Considering that we are dealing with a small dataset, we use a split ratio of 60/20/20%. Remember that for larger datasets, the split ratio usually changes to 98/1/1%.

The outputs of the function are four matrices: **X** divided into two subsets (train and test) and **Y** divided into two corresponding subsets.

```
print(X_train.shape, X_test.shape, Y_train.shape, Y_test.shape)
```

By printing the shape of all 4 matrices, it is possible to confirm that the size of the test subset (both **X** and **Y**) is 20% of the total size of the original dataset (150 * 0.2 = 30), while the size of the train set is the remaining 80%:

```
(120,4) (30,4) (120,1) (30,1)
```

6. To create a validation set (dev set), we will use the **train_test_split** function to divide the train sets obtained in the last step. However, before doing so, to obtain a dev set of shape same as that of the test, it is necessary to calculate the proportion of the size of the test set over the size of the train set. This value will be used as the **test_size** for the next step:

   ```
   dev_size = 30/120
   ```

   Here, 30 is the size of the test set created and 120 is the size of the train set that will be further split. The result from this operation is 0.25.

7. Use the **train_test_split** function to divide the train set into two subsets (train and dev sets). Use the result from the operation in the last step as the **test_size**:

   ```
   X_train, X_dev, Y_train, Y_dev = train_test_split(X_train, Y_train, test_
   size = 0.25)
   ```

   The result from the entire exercise are 6 different subsets of the following shapes:

   ```
   X_train = (90,4)
   Y_train = (90,1)
   X_dev = (30,4)
   Y_dev = (30,1)
   X_test = (30,4)
   Y_test = (30,1)
   ```

Congratulations! You have successfully split the dataset into three subsets to develop efficient machine learning projects. Feel free to test different split ratios.

In conclusion, the split ratio to partition data is not fixed, and should be decided by taking into account the amount of data available, the type of algorithm to be used, and the distribution of the data.

Cross Validation

Cross validation is also a procedure used to partition data by resampling the data used to train and validate the model. It consists of a parameter, K, that represents the number of groups in which the dataset will be divided.

Due to this, the procedure is also referred to as K-fold cross-validation, where K is usually replaced by the selected number. For instance, a model created using a 10-fold cross-validation procedure signifies a model where data is divided into 10 subgroups. The procedure of cross validation is illustrated below:

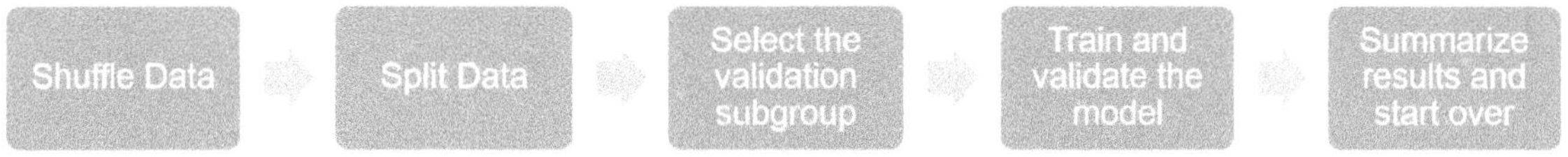

Figure 3.3: Cross-validation procedure

The preceding diagram displays the general procedure followed during cross validation:

1. Data is first shuffled randomly, considering that the process is repeated.
2. Data is split into K subgroups.
3. The validation/testing set is selected as one of the subgroups that was created. The rest of the subgroups become the training set.
4. The model is trained over the training set, as usual. The model is evaluated using the validation/testing dataset.
5. The result from that iteration is saved. The hyperparameters are tuned based on the results, and the process starts again by reshuffling the data. The process is repeated K number of times.

According to the preceding steps, the dataset is divided into K sets and the model is trained K times. Each time, one set is selected as the dev set, and the remaining sets are used for the training process.

Cross-validation can be done using a three-split approach or a two-split one. For the former, the dataset is initially divided into training and testing sets, after which the training set is divided using cross-validation to create different configurations of training and validation sets. The latter approach, on the other hand, uses cross-validation over the entire dataset.

The popularity of cross-validation is due to its capacity to build "unbiased" models that will perform well over unseen data. Moreover, it is also popular because it allows you to build highly effective models out of a small dataset.

There is no exact science to choosing the value for K, but it is important to consider that lower values for K tend to decrease variance and increase bias, while higher K values result in the opposite behavior. Also, the lower the K, the less expensive the processes, which results in faster running times.

> **Note**
>
> The concepts of variance and bias will be explained later.

Exercise 11: Using Cross-Validation to Partition the Train Set into a Training and a Validation Set

In this exercise, we will be performing data partition over the **iris** dataset using the cross validation method.

1. Open a Jupyter Notebook to implement this exercise.
2. Load the **iris** dataset as per the previous exercise and create the Pandas DataFrames containing the features and target matrices:

```
from sklearn.datasets import load_iris
import pandas as pd

iris_data = load_iris()
X = pd.DataFrame(iris_data.data)
Y = pd.DataFrame(iris_data.target)
```

3. Split the data into training and testing sets, using the **train_test_split** function that you learned about in the previous exercise:

```
from sklearn.model_selection import train_test_split
X, X_test, Y, Y_test = train_test_split(X, Y, test_size = 0.2)
```

4. Import the **KFold** class from scikit-learn's **model_selection** package:

```
from sklearn.model_selection import KFold
```

5. Initialize the **KFold** class with a 10-fold configuration:

```
kf = Kfold(n_splits = 10)
```

6. Then, apply the split method to the data in **X**. This method will output the index of the instances to be used as training and validation sets. The method creates 10 different split configurations. Save the output in a variable named **splits**:

```
splits = kf.split(X)
```

   Note that it is not necessary to run the **split** method over the data in **Y**, as the method only saves the index numbers, which will be the same for **X** and **Y**. The actual splitting is handled next.

7. Perform a **for** loop that will go through the different split configurations. In the loop body, create the variables that will hold the data for the training and validation sets. Use the following code snippet:

```
for train_index, dev_index in splits:
X_train, X_dev = X.iloc[train_index], X.iloc[dev_index]
Y_train, Y_dev = Y.iloc[train_index], Y.iloc[dev_index]
```

   The **for** loop goes through K number of configurations. In the body of the loop, the data is split using the index numbers.

> **Note**
>
> The code to train and evaluate the model should be written inside the loop body, given that the objective of the cross-validation procedure is to train and validate the model using the different split configurations.

Congratulations! You have successfully performed a cross-validation split over a sample dataset.

In conclusion, cross-validation is a procedure used to shuffle and split the data into training and validation sets so that the process of training and validating is done each time over different data, thus achieving a model with low bias.

Activity 8: Data Partition over a Handwritten Digit Dataset

Your company specializes in recognizing handwritten characters. It wants to improve the recognition of digits, which is why they have gathered a dataset of 1,797 handwritten digits from 0 to 9. The images have already been converted into their numeric representation, and so they have provided you with the dataset to split it into training/validation/testing sets. You can choose to either perform conventional splitting or cross-validation. Follow these steps to complete this activity:

1. Import the toy dataset **`digits`** using scikit-learn's **`datasets`** package and create a Pandas DataFrame containing the features and target matrices.
2. Choose the appropriate approach for splitting the dataset and split it.

> **Note**
>
> The solution for this activity can be found on page 196. Also, note that the results may vary depending on the approach and ratios used to spilt the dataset.

Evaluation Metrics

Model evaluation is indispensable for creating effective models that not only perform well over the data that was used to train the model but also generalize to unseen data. The task of evaluating the model is especially easy when dealing with supervised learning problems, where there is a ground truth that can be compared against the prediction of the model.

Determining the accuracy percentage of the model is crucial for its application to unseen data that does not have a label class to compare to. Considering this, for example, a model with an accuracy of 98% may allow the user to assume that the odds of having an accurate prediction are high, and hence the model should be trusted.

The evaluation of performance, as mentioned previously, should be done over the validation set (dev set) for fine-tuning the model, and over the test set for determining the expected performance of the selected model over unseen data.

Evaluation Metrics for Classification Tasks

A classification task refers to a model where the class label is a discrete value, as mentioned previously. Considering this, the most common measure to evaluate the performance of such tasks is by calculating the accuracy of the model, which involves comparing the actual prediction to the real value. Even though this may be an appropriate metric in many cases, there are several others to consider as well before choosing one.

The most commonly used performance metrics are explained as follows.

Confusion Matrix

The **confusion matrix** is a table that contains the performance of the model, and is described as follows:

- The columns represent the instances that belong to a predicted class.
- The rows refer to the instances that actually belong to that class (ground truth).

The configuration that confusion matrices present allow the user to quickly spot the areas in which the model is having greater difficulty. Take, for instance, the following table:

Prediction / Ground Truth	number 6	any other number
number 6	556	44
any other number	123	477

Figure 3.4: A confusion matrix of a digit classifier that recognizes the number 6

The following can be observed from the preceding table:

- By summing up the values in the first row, it is possible to know that there are 600 instances with the `number 6`. However, from those 600 instances, the model predicted 556 as the `number 6` and 44 as `any other number`. Hence, the model's ability to predict true instances has a correctness level of 92.6%.
- Regarding the second row, there are also 600 instances that are `any other number`. Nevertheless, out of those 600, the model predicted that 23 of them were the `number 6` and 477 were `any other number`. The model successfully predicted the false instances 79.5% of the time.

Based on these statements, it is possible to conclude that the model is performing at its worst when classifying the instances that are `any other number`.

Considering that the rows in a confusion matrix refer to the occurrence or non-occurrence of an event, and the columns refer to the model's predictions, the values in the confusion matrix are explained as follows, and are shown in the following table.

- **True positives**: Refers to the instances that the model correctly classified as positive to the event in question. For example, the instances correctly classified as the `number 6`.
- **False positives**: Refers to the instances that the model incorrectly classified as positive to the event. For example, the `any other number` instances that were incorrectly classified as the `number 6`.
- **True negatives**: Represents the instances that were correctly classified as negative to the event. For example, the instances correctly classified as `any other number`.
- **False negatives**: Refers to the instances incorrectly classified as negative to the event. For example, the `number 6` instances that were incorrectly predicted as `any other number`.

	Predicted: True	Predicted: False
Actual: True	TP	FN
Actual: False	FP	TN

Figure 3.5: A table showing confusion matrix values

Accuracy

Accuracy, as explained previously, measures the model's ability to correctly classify all instances. Although this is considered to be one of the simplest ways of measuring performance, it may not always be a useful metric when the objective of the study is to minimize/maximize the occurrence of one class independently of its performance over other classes.

The accuracy level of the confusion matrix from Figure 3.4 is measured as follows:

$$Accuracy = \frac{(TP + TN)}{m} = 0.8608 \approx 86\%$$

Figure 3.6: An equation showing the calculation of accuracy

Here, m is the total number of instances.

The 86% accuracy refers to the overall performance of the model in classifying both class labels.

Precision

This metric measures the model's ability to correctly classify positive labels (the label that represents the occurrence of the event) by comparing it to the total number of instances predicted as positive.

This is represented by the ratio between the *true positives* and the sum of the *true positives* and *false positives*, as shown in the following equation:

$$Precision = \frac{TP}{TP + FP}$$

Figure 3.7: An equation showing the calculation of precision

The precision metric is only applicable to binary classification tasks, where there are only two class labels (for instance, true or false). It could also be applied to multiclass tasks considering that the classes are converted into two (for instance, being a 6 or being any other number), where one of the classes refers to the instances that have a condition while the other refers to those that do not.

For the example in Figure 3.4, the precision of the model is equal to 81.8%.

Recall

The recall metric measures the number of correctly predicted positive labels against all positive labels. This is represented by the ratio between *true positives* and the sum of *true positives* and *false negatives*:

$$Recall = \frac{TP}{TP + FN}$$

Figure 3.8: An equation showing the calculation of recall

Again, this measure should be applied over two label classes.

The value of recall for the example in Figure 3.4 is 92.6%, which when compared to the other two metrics, represents the highest performance of the model. The decision to choose one metric or the other will depend on the purpose of the study, which will be further explained later.

Exercise 12: Calculating Different Evaluation Metrics over a Classification Task

In this exercise, we will be using the **breast cancer** toy dataset to calculate the evaluation metrics using the scikit-learn library.

1. Open a Jupyter Notebook to implement this exercise.
2. For the following exercise, the **breast cancer** toy dataset will be used. This dataset contains the final diagnosis (malignant or benign) of the analysis of masses found in the breasts of 569 women. Use the following code to load and split the dataset, which is the same as what we did for the previous exercises:

```
from sklearn.datasets import load_breast_cancer
data = load_breast_cancer()

import pandas as pd
X = pd.DataFrame(data.data)
Y = pd.DataFrame(data.target)

from sklearn.model_selection import train_test_split
X_train, X_test, Y_train, Y_test = train_test_split(X,Y, test_size = 0.1,
random_state = 0)
```

   Note that the dataset is divided into two subsets (train and test sets) mainly because the purpose of this exercise is to learn how to calculate the evaluation metrics using the scikit-learn package.

> **Note**
>
> The **random_state** parameter is used to set a seed that will ensure the same results every time you run the code. This guarantees that you will get the same results as the ones reflected in this exercise.
>
> Different numbers can be used as the seed; however, use the same number as suggested in the exercises and activities of this chapter to get the same results as the ones shown.

3. Train a decision tree over the train set. Then, use the model to predict the class label over the test set. Use the following code:

```
from sklearn import tree
model = tree.DecisionTreeClassifier(random_state = 0)
model = model.fit(X_train, Y_train)
```

```
Y_pred = model.predict(X_test)
```

As a general explanation, the model is first initialized using a **random_state** to set a seed. Then, the **fit** method is used to train the model using the data from the train sets (both **X** and **Y**). Finally, the **predict** method is used to trigger the predictions over the data in the test set (only **X**). The data from **Y_test** will be used to compare the predictions to the ground truth.

> **Note**
>
> The steps for training a supervised learning model will be explained further in later chapters.

4. Use scikit-learn to construct a confusion matrix. See the following code:

```
from sklearn.metrics import confusion_matrix
confusion_matrix = confusion_matrix(Y_test, Y_pred)
```

The result is displayed as follows, where the ground truth is measured against the prediction:

```
[ [21, 1],
[6, 29] ]
```

5. Calculate the accuracy, precision, and recall of the model, by comparing **Y_test** and **Y_pred**:

```
from sklearn.metrics import accuracy_score, precision_score, recall_score

accuracy = accuracy_score(Y_test, Y_pred)
precision = precision_score(Y_test, Y_pred)
recall = recall_score(Y_test, Y_pred)
```

The results are displayed as follows:

```
Accuracy = 0.8771
Precision = 0.9666
Recall = 0.8285
```

Given that the positive labels are those where the mass is malignant, it can be concluded that the instances that the model predicts as malignant have a high probability (96.6%) of being malignant, but for the instances predicted as benign, the model has a 17.15% (100%–82.85%) probability of being wrong.

Congratulations! You have successfully calculated evaluation metrics over a classification task.

Choosing an Evaluation Metric

There are several metrics that can be used to measure the performance of a model over classification tasks, and selecting the right one is key for building a model that performs exceptionally well for the purpose of the study.

Previously, the importance of understanding the purpose of the study was mentioned as a useful insight to determine the preprocessing techniques required to perform over the dataset. Moreover, the purpose of the study is also useful to determine the ideal metric to measure the performance of the model.

Why is the purpose of the study important for selecting the evaluation metric? Because by understanding the main goal of the study, it is possible to decide whether it is important to focus attention on the overall performance of the model or only on one of the class labels.

For instance, a model that has been created to recognize when birds are present in a picture does not need to perform well in recognizing which other animals are present in the picture as long as it does not classify them as birds. This means that the model needs to focus on improving the performance of correctly classifying birds only.

On the other hand, for a model that has been created to recognize hand-written characters, where no one character is more important than another, the ideal metric would be the one that measures the overall accuracy of the model.

What would happen if more than one metric is selected? It would become difficult to arrive at the best performance of the model, considering that measuring two metrics simultaneously can result in needing different approaches to improve results.

Evaluation Metrics for Regression Tasks

Considering that regression tasks are those where the final output is continuous, without a fixed number of output labels, the comparison between the ground truth and the prediction is based on the proximity of the values rather than on them having exactly the same values. For instance, when predicting house prices, a model that predicts a value of USD 299,846 for a house valued at USD 300,000 can be considered to be a good model.

The two metrics most commonly used for evaluating the accuracy of continuous variables are the **Mean Absolute Error** (**MAE**) and the **Root Mean Squared Error** (**RMSE**), which are explained here:

- **Mean Absolute Error**: This metric measures the average absolute difference between a prediction and the ground truth, without taking into account the direction of the error. The formulae to calculate the MAE is as follows:

$$MAE = \frac{1}{m} * \sum_{i=1}^{m} |y_i - \hat{y}_i|$$

Figure 3.9: An equation showing the calculation of MAE

Here, *m* refers to the total number of instances, *y* is the ground truth, and *y_hat* is the predicted value.

- **Root Mean Squared Error**: This is a quadratic metric that also measures the average magnitude of error between the ground truth and the prediction. As the name suggests, the RMSE is the square root of the average of the squared differences, as shown in the following formula:

$$RMSE = \sqrt{\frac{1}{m} * \sum_{i=1}^{m} (y_i - \hat{y}_i)^2}$$

Figure 3.10: An equation showing the calculation of RMSE

Both these metrics express the average error, in a range from 0 to infinity, where the lower the values, the better the performance of the model. The main difference between these two metrics is that the MAE assigns the same weight of importance to all errors, while the RMSE squares the error, assigning higher weights to larger errors.

Considering this, the RMSE metric is especially useful in cases where larger errors should be penalized, meaning that outliers are taken into account in the measurement of performance. For instance, the RMSE metric can be used when a value that is off by 4 is more than twice as bad as being off by 2. The MAE, on the other hand, is used when a value that is off by 4 is just twice as bad as a value off by 2.

Exercise 13: Calculating Evaluation Metrics over a Regression Task

In this exercise, we will be calculating evaluation metrics over a model trained using linear regression. We will use the **boston** toy dataset for this purpose.

1. Open a Jupyter Notebook to implement this exercise.
2. For the following exercise, the **boston** toy dataset will be used. This dataset contains data of 506 house prices in Boston. Use the following code to load and split the dataset, the same as we did for the previous exercises:

```
from sklearn.datasets import load_boston
data = load_boston()

import pandas as pd
X = pd.DataFrame(data.data)
Y = pd.DataFrame(data.target)

from sklearn.model_selection import train_test_split
X_train, X_test, Y_train, Y_test = train_test_split(X,Y, test_size = 0.1,
random_state = 0)
```

3. Train a linear regression over the train set. Then, use the model to predict the class label over the test set. Use the following code:

```
from sklearn import linear_model
model = linear_model.LinearRegression()
model = model.fit(X_train, Y_train)

Y_pred = model.predict(X_test)
```

   As a general explanation, the model is first initialized. Then, the **fit** method is used to train the model using the data from the train sets (both **X** and **Y**). Finally, the **predict** method is used to trigger the predictions over the data in the test set (only **X**). The data from **Y_test** will be used to compare the predictions to the ground truth.

4. Calculate both the MAE and RMSE metrics:

```
import numpy as np
from sklearn.metrics import mean_absolute_error, mean_squared_error

MAE = mean_absolute_error(Y_test, Y_pred)
RMSE = np.sqrt(mean_squared_error(Y_test, Y_pred))
```

The results are displayed as follows:

```
MAE = 3.9343
RMSE = 6.4583
```

> **Note**
>
> The scikit-learn library allows you to directly calculate the MSE. To calculate the RMSE, the square root of the value obtained from the **mean_squared_error()** function is calculated. By using the square root, we ensure that the values from MAE and RMSE are comparable.

From the results, it is possible to conclude that the model performs well over the test set, considering that both values are close to zero. Nevertheless, this also means that the performance can still be improved.

Congratulations! You have successfully calculated evaluation metrics on a regression task.

Activity 9: Evaluating the Performance of the Model Trained over a Handwritten Dataset

You continue to work on improving the model to recognize handwritten digits. The team has built a model and they want you to evaluate the performance of the model. Follow these steps to complete this activity:

1. Import the **digits** toy dataset using scikit-learn's **datasets** package and create a Pandas DataFrame containing the features and target matrices.
2. Split the data into training and testing sets. Use 20% as the size of the testing set.
3. Train a decision tree over the train set. Then, use the model to predict the class label over the test set.

> **Note**
>
> To train the Decision Tree, revisit Exercise 12.

4. Use scikit-learn to construct a confusion matrix.
5. Calculate the accuracy of the model.
6. Calculate the precision and recall. Considering that both the precision and recall can only be calculated over binary data, assume that we are only interested in classifying instances as **`number 6`** or **`any other number`**.

   To be able to calculate the precision and recall, use the following code to convert **`Y_test`** and **`Y_pred`** into a one-hot vector. A one-hot vector consists of a vector that only contains zeros and ones. For this activity, the 0 represents the *number* 6, and the 1 represents **`any other number`**. This converts the class labels (**`Y_test`** and **`Y_pred`**) into binary data, meaning that there are only two possible outcomes instead of 10 different ones.

   Then, calculate the precision and recall using the new variables:

```
Y_test_2 = Y_test[:]
Y_test_2[Y_test_2 != 6] = 1
Y_test_2[Y_test_2 == 6] = 0

Y_pred_2 = Y_pred
Y_pred_2[Y_pred_2 != 6] = 1
Y_pred_2[Y_pred_2 == 6] = 0
```

> **Note**
>
> The solution for this activity can be found on page 198.

You should obtain the following values as the output:

```
Accuracy = 84.72%
Precision = 98.41%
Recall = 98.10%
```

Error Analysis

Building an average model, as explained so far, is surprisingly easy through the use of the scikit-learn library. Considering this, the key aspects to building an exceptional model come from the analysis and decision making on the part of the researcher.

As we have seen so far, some of the most important tasks are choosing and pre-processing the dataset, determining the purpose of the study, and selecting the appropriate evaluation metric. After handling all of this and taking into account that a model needs to be fine-tuned in order to reach the highest standards, most data scientists recommend training a simple model, regardless of the hyperparameters, to get the study started.

Error analysis is then introduced as a very useful methodology to turn an average model into an exceptional one. As the name suggests, it consists of analyzing the errors among the different subsets of the dataset in order to target the condition that is affecting the model on a greater scale.

Bias, Variance, and Data Mismatch

To understand the different conditions that may affect a machine learning model, it is important to understand what a **Bayes Error** is. A Bayes Error, also known as the **irreducible error**, is the lowest possible error that can be achieved.

Before the improvements in technology and artificial intelligence, the Bayes Error was considered to be the lowest possible error achievable by humans (**Human Error**). For instance, for a process that most humans achieve with an error rate of 0.1, but top experts achieve with an error rate of 0.05, the Bayes Error would be 0.05.

Nevertheless, nowadays, Bayes Error is redefined as being the lowest possible error that machines can achieve, which is unknown considering that, as humans, we can only understand as far as Human Error goes. Due to this, when using the Bayes Error to analyze errors, it is not possible to know the lowest limit once the model is below the Human Error.

The following diagram is useful for analyzing the error rates among the different sets of data and determining the condition that is affecting the model in greater proportion. The purpose of the diagram is to find the errors that differ to a greater extent to each other so that the model can be diagnosed and improved accordingly. Moreover, it is important to highlight that the value of the errors for each set is calculated by subtracting the evaluation metrics from 100% or 1 (depending on the scale on which the performance was measured). For instance, a performance of 86% (0.86) over the test set translates into a Test Set Error of 14% (0.14):

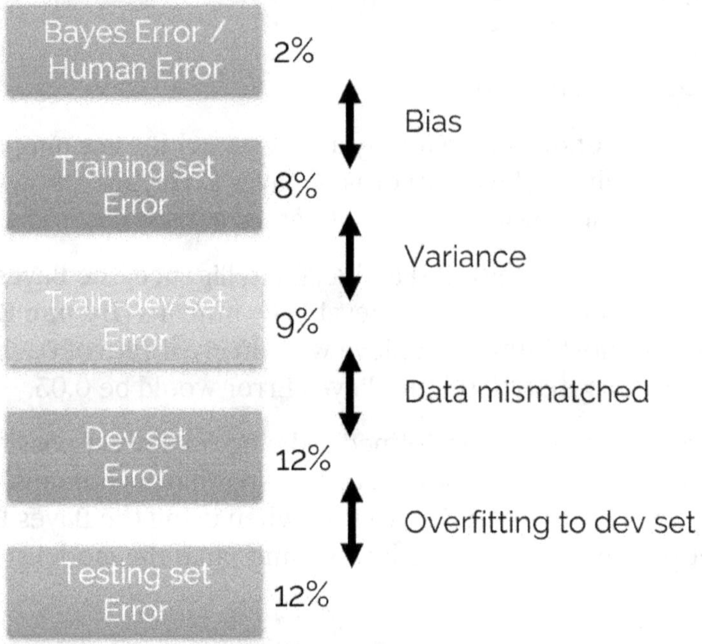

Figure 3.11: Error analysis methodology

The decision to determine which condition is affecting the model is done by taking the error rate of a set and subtracting the value of the error rate of the set above. The two sets with the highest numerical difference are the ones to look into to diagnose the model. However, it is important to consider that negative differences should not be taken into account as the main idea behind error analysis is to bring down error rates as much as possible.

According to this, when the error rate above is lower, the condition explained in the table serves to identify the issue and to set the measures to improve the results. On the other hand, if the error rate above is higher, the problem is not between those two sets, but the two sets above.

For example, the values in the preceding diagram show that the greatest difference is located between the Bayes Error and the Training set error, considering that those two errors have a greater (positive) numerical distance when subtracting one from the other. This helps to determine that the model is suffering from *high bias*.

> **Note**
>
> The train/dev set is a combination of data in the training and the validation (dev) sets. It is usually of the same shape of the dev set and it contains the same amount of data from both sets.

An explanation of each of the conditions is as follows, along with some techniques to avoid/fix them:

- **Bias**: Also known as *underfitting*, bias occurs when the model is not generalizing to the training set, which translates into the model performing poorly for all three sets (training, validation, and testing sets) as well as for unseen data.

  Underfitting is the easiest condition to detect and it usually requires changing to a different algorithm that may be a better fit for the data available. With regard to neural networks, it can be fixed by constructing a bigger network or by training for longer periods of time.

- **Variance**: Also known as *overfitting*, this condition refers to the model's inability to perform well over data different than that of the training set. It basically means that the model has overfitted to the training data by learning the details and outliers of the data, without making any generalizations. A model suffering from overfitting will not perform well over the dev or test sets, or over unseen data.

  Overfitting can be fixed by tuning the different hyperparameters of the algorithm, often with the objective of simplifying the algorithm's approximation of the data. For instance, for decision trees, it can be addressed by pruning the tree to delete some of the details learned from the training data. In neural networks, on the other hand, it can be addressed by adding regularization techniques that seek to reduce some of the neuron's influence in the overall result.

  Additionally, adding more data to the training set can also help the model avoid high variance.

- **Data mismatch**: This occurs when the training and validation sets do not follow the same distribution. This affects the model as although it generalizes based on the training data, this generalization does not describe the data found in the validation set. For instance, a model created to describe landscape photographs may suffer from data mismatch if it is trained using high definition images, while the actual images that will be used once the model has been built are unprofessional.

  Logically, the best way to avoid data mismatch is to make sure that the sets follow the same distribution. For example, you can do this by shuffling together the images from both sources (professional and unprofessional images) and then dividing them into the different sets.

  Nevertheless, in the case that there is not enough data that follows the same distribution of unseen data (data that will be used in the future), it is highly recommended to create the dev and test sets entirely out of that data and add the remaining to the large training set. From the preceding example, the unprofessional images should be used to create the dev and test sets, adding the remaining ones to the training set, along with the professional images.

  This helps to train a model with a set that contains enough images to make a generalization, but it uses data with the same distribution as the unseen data to fine-tune the model.

  Finally, if the data from all sets does in fact come from the same distribution, this condition actually refers to a problem of high variance and should be handled as such.

- **Overfitting to the dev set**: Lastly, similar to the variance condition, this occurs when the model is not generalizing but instead is fitting the dev set too well.

  It should be addressed using the same approaches that were explained for high variance.

Exercise 14: Calculating the Error Rate over Different Sets of Data

In this exercise, we will calculate error rates for a model trained using a decision tree. We will use the breast cancer dataset for this purpose.

1. Open a Jupyter Notebook to implement this exercise.
2. For the following exercise, the `breast cancer` dataset will be used. Use the following code to load the dataset and create the DataFrames containing the features and target matrices:

```
from sklearn.datasets import load_breast_cancer
```

```
data = load_breast_cancer()

import pandas as pd
X = pd.DataFrame(data.data)
Y = pd.DataFrame(data.target)
```

3. Split the dataset into training, validation, and testing sets:

```
from sklearn.model_selection import train_test_split

X_new, X_test, Y_new, Y_test = train_test_split(X, Y, test_size = 0.1,
random_state = 101)

X_train, X_dev, Y_train, Y_dev = train_test_split(X_new, Y_new, test_size
= 0.11, random_state = 101)
```

4. Create a train/dev set that combines data from both the training and validation sets:

```
import numpy as np
np.random.seed(101)

indices_train = np.random.randint(0, len(X_train), 25)
indices_dev = np.random.randint(0, len(X_dev), 25)

X_train_dev = pd.concat([X_train.iloc[indices_train,:], X_dev.
iloc[indices_dev,:]])

Y_train_dev = pd.concat([Y_train.iloc[indices_train,:], Y_dev.
iloc[indices_dev,:]])
```

First, we import NumPy and set a random seed. Next, the NumPy function **random.randint()** is used to select random indices from the **X_train** set. To do that, 25 random integers are generated in a range between 0 and the total length of **X_train**. The same process is used to generate the random indices of the dev set. Finally, a new variable is created to store the selected values of **X_train** and **X_dev**, as well as a variable to store the corresponding values from **Y_train** and **Y_dev**.

The variables that have been created contain 25 instances/labels from the train set and 25 instances/labels from the dev set.

5. Train a decision tree over the train set. Use the following code:

```
from sklearn import tree

model = tree.DecisionTreeClassifier(random_state = 101)
model = model.fit(X_train, Y_train)
```

6. Use the **predict** method to generate the predictions for all of your sets (train, train/dev, dev, and test). Next, considering that the objective of the study is to maximize the model's ability to predict all malignant cases, calculate the recall scores for all predictions. Store all of the scores in a variable named **scores**:

```
from sklearn.metrics import recall_score
X_sets = [X_train, X_train_dev, X_dev, X_test]
Y_sets = [Y_train, Y_train_dev, Y_dev, Y_test]

scores = []
for i in range(0, len(X_sets)):
  pred = model.predict(X_sets[i])
  score = recall_score(Y_sets[i], pred)
  scores.append(score)
```

The error rates for all of the sets of data are shown in the following table:

Set	Error
Bayes Error/Human Error	0
Training set Error	0
Train/Dev set Error	0.0295
Dev set Error	0.0667
Testing set Error	0.0286

Figure 3.12: Error rates from the Breast Cancer model

Here, the Bayes Error was assumed as 0 considering that the classification between a malignant and a benign mass is done by taking a biopsy of the mass.

From the preceding table, it can be concluded that the model performs exceptionally well for the purpose of the study, considering that all error rates are close to 0, which is the lowest possible error.

The highest difference in error rates is found between the train/dev set and the dev set, which refers to data mismatch. However, taking into account that all the datasets come from the same distribution, this condition is considered a high variance issue, where adding more data to the training set should help reduce the error rate.

Congratulations! You have successfully calculated the error rate of all subsets of the data.

Activity 10: Performing Error Analysis over a Model Trained to Recognize Handwritten Digits

Based on the different metrics that you have provided to your team to measure the performance of the model, they have selected accuracy as the ideal metric. Considering this, your team has asked you to perform error analysis to determine how the model could be improved. Follow these steps to achieve this:

1. Import the **`digits`** toy dataset using scikit-learn's **`datasets`** package and create a Pandas DataFrame containing the features and target matrices.
2. Split the data into training, validation, and testing sets. Use 0.1 as the size of the test set, and an equivalent number to build a validation set of the same shape.
3. Create a train/dev set for both the features and target values that contains 89 instances/labels of the train set and 89 instances/labels of the dev set.
4. Train a decision tree over that training set data.
5. Calculate the error rate for all sets of data, and determine which condition is affecting the performance of the model.

> **Note**
>
> The solution for this activity can be found on page 199.

Summary

When developing machine learning models, one of the main goals is for the model to be capable of generalizing so that it can be applicable to future unseen data, instead of just learning a set of instances very well but performing poorly on new data. Accordingly, a methodology for validation and testing was explained in this chapter, which involved splitting the data into three sets: a training set, a dev set, and a test set. This approach eliminates the risk of bias. After this, the chapter covered how to evaluate the performance of a model for both classification and regression problems. Finally, we covered how to analyze the performance and perform error analysis for each of the sets and detect the condition affecting the model's performance.

In the next chapter, we will focus on applying different algorithms to a real-life dataset, with the underlying objective of applying the steps learned here to choose the best performing algorithm for the case study.

4

Supervised Learning Algorithms: Predict Annual Income

Learning Objectives

By the end of this chapter, you will be able to:

- Identify the purpose of a case study
- Explain the methodologies of three different supervised learning algorithms used for classification
- Solve a supervised learning classification problem using different algorithms
- Perform error analysis by comparing the results of different algorithms
- Identify the algorithm with the best performance

This chapter describes a practical implementation of a supervised algorithm to a real-world dataset.

Introduction

In the previous chapter, we covered the key steps involved in working with a supervised learning data problem. These steps aim to create high performance algorithms, as explained previously. This chapter focuses on applying different algorithms to a real-life dataset, with the underlying objective of applying the steps that we learned previously to choose the best performing algorithm for the case study. Considering this, you will analyze and preprocess a dataset, and then create three models using different algorithms. These models will be compared to one another, in order to measure performance.

Exploring the Dataset

Real-life applications are crucial for cementing knowledge. Therefore, this chapter consists of a real-life case study involving a classification task, where the key steps that you learned in the previous chapter will be applied in order to select the best performing model.

To accomplish this, the Census Income Dataset will be used, which is available at the UC Irvine Machine Learning Repository.

> **Note**
>
> To download the dataset, visit http://archive.ics.uci.edu/ml/datasets/Census+Income.

Once you have located the repository, follow these steps to download the dataset:

1. First, click the `Data Folder` link.
2. For this chapter, the data available under `adult.data` will be used. Once you are inside of the link, you should be able to see the data.
3. Right-click it and select **Save as**.
4. Save it as a `.csv` file.

> **Note**
>
> Open the file and add header names over each column to make the pre-preprocessing easier. For instance, the first column should have the header **Age**, as per the features available in the dataset. These can be seen in the preceding link, under **Attribute Information**.

Understanding the Dataset

To build a model that fits the data accurately, it is important to understand the different details of the dataset, as mentioned in previous chapters.

First, the data that's available is revised to understand the size of the dataset and the type of supervised learning task to be developed: classification or regression. Next, the purpose of the study is clearly defined, even if it is obvious. For supervised learning, the purpose is closely linked to the class labels. Finally, each feature is analyzed, so that we can be aware of their type for preprocessing purposes.

The Census Income Dataset is a collection of demographical data from adults, which was obtained from the 1994 Census Dataset. For this chapter, only the data available under the `adult.data` link has been used. The dataset consists of 32,561 instances, 14 features, and 1 binary class label. Considering that the class labels are discrete, our task is to achieve a classification.

Through this quick evaluation of data, it is possible to observe that some features present missing values in the form of a question mark. This is common when dealing with datasets that are available online and should be handled by replacing the symbol with an empty value (not a space). Other common forms of missing values are the `NULL` value and a dash.

To edit missing values symbols in Excel, use the **Replace** functionality, as follows:

1. **Find what**: Input the symbol that is being used to signify a missing value (for example, `?`).
2. **Replace with**: Leave it blank (do not enter a space).

This way, once we import the dataset into the code, NumPy will be able to find the missing values so that it can handle them.

The prediction task for this dataset involves determining whether a person earns over 50K dollars a year. According to this, the two possible outcome labels are `>50K` (greater than 50K) or `<=50K` (less than, or equal to 50K).

A brief explanation of each of the features in the dataset is shown in the following table:

Feature	Type	Note	Relevant
`age`	Quantitative (continuous)	The age of the individual.	Yes
`workclass`	Qualitative (nominal)	The type of employment of the individual.	Yes
`fnlwgt`	Quantitative (continuous)	The number of people the census takers believe the individual represents.	No; the values were subjective to the census taker
`education`	Qualitative (ordinal)	The highest education level achieved, by the individual.	No; the **`education-num`** feature represents the same information, but is preferred because it is presented in numerical form
`education-num`	Quantitative (continuous)	The highest education level achieved in numerical form.	Yes
`marital-status`	Qualitative (nominal)	The marital status of the individual.	Yes
`occupation`	Qualitative (nominal)	The current occupation of the individual.	Yes
`relationship`	Qualitative (nominal)	A relationship value that represents the individual.	No; this feature is ignored since its purpose is not clear.
`race`	Qualitative (nominal)	The race of the individual.	Although (in some cases) this feature may be relevant, for ethical reasons, it will be excluded from the study*

`sex`	Qualitative (nominal)	The gender of the individual.	Although (in some cases) this feature may be relevant, for ethical reasons, it will be excluded from the study*
`capital-gain`	Quantitative (continuous)	All of the individual's recorded capital gains.	Yes
`capital-loss`	Quantitative (continuous)	All of the individual's recorded capital loss.	Yes
`hours-per-week`	Quantitative (continuous)	The number of hours that the individual works per week.	Yes
`native-country`	Qualitative (nominal)	The native country of the individual.	Yes

Figure 4.1: Dataset feature analysis

> **Note**
>
> *Publisher's Note: Gender and race would have impacted the earning potential of an individual at the date this study was conducted. However, for the purpose of this chapter, we have decided to exclude these categories from our exercises and activities.
>
> We recognize that due to biases and discriminatory practices, it is impossible to separate issues such as gender, race, and educational and vocational opportunities. The removal of certain features from our dataset in the preprocessing stage of these exercises is not intended to ignore the issues, nor the valuable work undertaken by organizations and individuals working in the civil rights sphere.
>
> We would strongly recommend the reader to consider the sociopolitical impacts of data and the way it is used, and to consider how past prejudices can be perpetuated by using historical data to introduce biases into new algorithms.

From the preceding table, it is possible to conclude the following:

- Five features are not relevant to the study: **fnlwgt**, **education**, **relationship**, **race**, and **sex**. These features must be deleted from the dataset before we proceed with the preprocessing and training of the model.
- Out of the remaining features, four are presented as qualitative values. Considering that many algorithms do not take qualitative features into account, the values should be represented in numerical form.

Using the concepts that we learned in previous chapters, the preceding statements, as well as the preprocessing process for handling outliers and missing values, can be taken care of. The following steps explain the logic of this process:

1. You need to import the dataset and drop the features that are irrelevant to the study.
2. You should check for missing values. Considering that the feature with the most missing values (occupation) has 1,843 instances, there will be no need to delete or replace the missing values, as they represent only 5% or less of the entire dataset.
3. You must convert the qualitative values to their numeric representations.
4. You should check for outliers. Upon using three standard deviations to detect outliers, the feature with the maximum number of outliers (capital-loss) will be the one with 1,470 instances, which is again less than 5% of the entire dataset. Again, they can be left unhandled.

The preceding process will convert the original dataset into a new dataset with 32,561 instances (since no instances were deleted), but with nine features and a class label. All values should be in their numerical forms.

> **Note**
>
> Make sure that you perform the preceding preprocessing step, as it will be used to begin all the activities in this chapter.

Naïve Bayes Algorithm

Naïve Bayes is a classification algorithm based on **Bayes' Theorem** that *naively* assumes independency between features and assigns the same weights (degree of importance) to all features. This means that the algorithm assumes that no single feature correlates to or affects another. For example, although weight and height are somehow correlated when predicting a person's age, the algorithm assumes that each feature is independent. Additionally, the algorithm considers all features equally important. For instance, even though the education degree may influence the earnings of a person to a greater degree than the number of children the person has, the algorithm still considers both features equally important.

Although real-life datasets contain features that are not equally important, nor independent, this algorithm is popular among scientists, as it performs surprisingly well over large datasets. Also, it is worth mentioning that thanks to its simplistic approach, it runs very quickly, allowing for its application to problems that require predictions in real time. Moreover, it is frequently used for text classification, as it commonly outperforms more complex algorithms.

How Does It Work?

The algorithm converts the input data into a summary of occurrences of each class label against each feature, which is then used to calculate the likelihood of one event (a class label), given a combination of features. Finally, this likelihood is normalized against the likelihood of the other class labels. The result is the probability of an instance belonging to each class label. The sum of the probabilities must be one, and the class label with a higher probability is the one that the algorithm chooses as the prediction.

Let's take, for example, the data presented in the following tables:

A

Weather	Temperature	Outcome
Sunny	Hot	Yes
Sunny	Cool	Yes
Rainy	Cold	No
Sunny	Hot	No
Mild	Cool	Yes
Mild	Cool	Yes
Sunny	Hot	Yes
Rainy	Cool	No
Rainy	Cold	Yes
Sunny	Hot	Yes

B

Weather	Yes	No
Sunny	4	1
Rainy	1	2
Mild	2	0

Temperature	Yes	No
Hot	3	1
Cool	3	1
Cold	1	1

Overall	Yes	No
	7	3

Figure 4.2: A) Input data, B) Occurrence count

The table on the left represents the data that is input to the algorithm used to build the model. The table on the right refers to the occurrence count that the algorithm uses implicitly to calculate the probabilities.

To calculate the likelihood of an event occurring when given a set of features, the algorithm multiplies the probability of the event occurring, given each individual feature, with the probability of the occurrence of the event independently of the rest of the features, as follows:

$$Likelihood\ [A_1|E] = P[A_1|E_1] * P[A_1|E_2] * P[A_1|E_n] * P[A_1]$$

Figure 4.3: Equation for the calculation of the likelihood of an event occurring

Here, A_1 refers to an event (one of the class labels) and E represents the set of features, where E_1 is the first feature and E_n is the last feature in the dataset. Note that the multiplication of these probabilities can only be made by assuming independency between features.

The preceding equation is calculated for all possible outcomes (all class labels), and then the normalized probability of each outcome is calculated, as follows:

$$P[A_1|E] = \frac{likelihood[A_1|E]}{(likelihood[A_1|E] + likelihood[A_2|E] + likelihood[A_n|E])}$$

Figure 4.4: Equation for the calculation of normalized probability of an event

For the example in *Figure 4.2*, given a new instance with weather equal to *sunny* and temperature equal to *cool*, the calculation of probabilities is as follows:

$$Likelihood[yes|sunny, cool] = \frac{4}{7} * \frac{3}{7} * \frac{7}{10} = 0.17$$

$$Likelihood[no|sunny, cool] = \frac{1}{3} * \frac{1}{3} * \frac{3}{10} = 0.03$$

$$P[yes|sunny, cool] = \frac{0.17}{0.17 + 0.03} = 0.85 \approx 85\%$$

$$P[no|sunny, cool] = \frac{0.03}{0.17 + 0.03} = 0.15 \approx 15\%$$

Figure 4.5: Calculation of the likelihood and probabilities for the example dataset

By looking at the preceding equations, it is possible to conclude that the prediction should be *yes*.

It is important to mention that for continuous features, the summary of occurrences is done by creating ranges. For instance, for a feature of price, the algorithm may count the number of instances with prices below 100K, as well as the instances with prices above 100K.

Moreover, the algorithm may encounter some issues if one value of a feature is never associated with one of the outcomes. This is an issue mainly because the probability of the outcome given that feature will be zero, which influences the entire calculation. In the preceding example, for predicting the outcome of an instance with weather equal to *mild* and temperature equal to *cool*, the probability of *no*, given the set of features will be equal to zero, considering that the probability of *no*, given *mild* weather, computes to zero, since there are no occurrences of *mild* weather when the outcome is *no*.

To avoid this, the **Laplace estimator** technique should be used. Here, the fractions representing the probability of the occurrence of an event given a feature, P[A|E1], are modified by adding 1 to the numerator while also adding the number of possible values of that feature to the denominator.

For this example, to perform a prediction for a new instance with a weather equal to *mild* and temperature equal to *cool*, using the Laplace estimator would be done as follows:

$$Likelihood[yes|mild, cool] = \frac{3}{10} * \frac{4}{10} * \frac{7}{10} = 0.084$$

$$Likelihood[no|mild, cool] = \frac{1}{6} * \frac{2}{6} * \frac{3}{10} = 0.016$$

$$P[yes|mild, cool] = \frac{0.084}{0.084 + 0.016} = 0.84 \approx 84\%$$

$$P[no|mild, cool] = \frac{0.016}{0.084 + 0.016} = 0.16 \approx 16\%$$

Figure 4.6: Calculation of the likelihood and probability using the Laplace estimator for the example dataset

Here, the fraction that calculates the occurrences of *yes*, given *mild* weather, goes from 2/7 to 3/10, as a result of the addition of 1 to the numerator and 3 (for *sunny*, *mild*, and *rainy*) to the denominator. The same goes for the other fractions that calculate the probability of the event, given a feature. Note that the fraction that calculates the probability of the event occurring independently of any feature is left unaltered.

Nevertheless, as you have learned so far, the scikit-learn library allows you to train models and then use them for predictions, without needing to hardcode the math.

Exercise 15: Applying the Naïve Bayes Algorithm

Now, let's apply the Naïve Bayes algorithm to a Fertility Dataset, which aims to determine whether the fertility level of an individual has been affected by their demographics, their environmental conditions, and their previous medical conditions.

> **Note**
>
> For the exercises and activities within this chapter, you will need to have Python 3.6, NumPy, Jupyter, Pandas, and scikit-learn installed on your system.

1. Download the Fertility Dataset from: http://archive.ics.uci.edu/ml/datasets/Fertility.

   Go to the link and click on **Data Folder**. Click on **fertility_Diagnosis.txt** and then right-click it and select **Save as**. Save it as a **.csv** file.

2. Open a Jupyter Notebook to implement this exercise.

3. Import **pandas** and read the **.csv** file that you downloaded in the first step. Make sure that you add the argument **header** equal to **None** to the **read_csv** function, considering that the dataset does not contain a header row:

   ```
   import pandas as pd
   data = pd.read_csv("datasets/fertility_Diagnosis.csv", header=None)
   ```

4. Split the data into **X** and **Y**, considering that the class label is found under the column with an index equal to 9. Use the following code:

   ```
   X = data.iloc[:,:9]
   Y = data.iloc[:,9]
   ```

5. Import scikit-learn's Gaussian Naïve Bayes class. Then, initialize it, and use the **fit** method to train the model using **X** and **Y**:

```
from sklearn.naive_bayes import GaussianNB
model = GaussianNB()
model.fit(X, Y)
```

   The output from running this script is as follows:

```
GaussianNB(priors=None, var_smoothing=1e-09)
```

   This states that the initialization of the class was successful. The information inside the parentheses represents the values used for the arguments that the class accepts, which are the hyperparameters.

   For instance, for the **GaussianNB** class, it is possible to set the prior probabilities to consider for the model and a smoothing argument that stabilizes variance. Nonetheless, the model was initialized without setting any arguments, which means that it will use the default values for each argument, which is **None** for the case of **priors** and is **1e-09** for the smoothing hyperparameter.

6. Finally, perform a prediction using the model that you trained before, for a new instance with the following values for each feature: -0.33, 0.69, 0, 1, 1, 0, 0.8, 0, 0.88.

   Use the following code:

```
pred = model.predict([[-0.33,0.69,0,1,1,0,0.8,0,0.88]])
print(pred)
```

   Note that we feed the values inside of double square brackets, considering that the **predict** function takes in the values for prediction as an array of arrays, where the first set of arrays corresponds to the list of new instances to predict and the second array refers to the list of features for each instance.

   From the preceding code, you should get a prediction equal to **N**.

Congratulations! You have successfully trained a Naïve Bayes model.

Activity 11: Training a Naïve Bayes Model for Our Census Income Dataset

To test different classification algorithms on a real-life dataset, consider the following scenario: you work for a bank and they have decided to implement a model that is able to predict a person's annual income and use that information to decide whether to approve a loan. You are given a dataset with 32,561 observations of previous clients, which you have already preprocessed. Your job is to build three different models over the dataset and determine which one best suits the case study. The first model to be built is a Gaussian Naïve Bayes model. Use the following steps to complete this activity:

1. Using the preprocessed Census Income Dataset, separate the features from the target by creating the variables `X` and `Y`.
2. Divide the dataset into training, validation, and testing sets, using a split ratio of 10%.

> **Note**
>
> When all three sets are created from the same dataset, it is not required to create an additional train/dev set to measure data mismatch. Moreover, note that it is OK to try a different split ratio, considering that the percentages explained in the previous chapter are not set in stone. Even though they tend to work well, it is important that you embrace experimentation in different levels when building machine learning models.

3. Import the Gaussian Naïve Bayes class, and then use the `fit` method to train the model over the training sets (`X_train` and `Y_train`).
4. Finally, perform a prediction using the model that you trained previously, for a new instance with the following values for each feature: 39, 6, 13, 4, 0, 2174, 0, 40, 38.

   The prediction for the individual should be equal to zero, meaning that the individual most likely has an income less than or equal to 50K.

> **Note**
>
> Use the same Jupyter Notebook for all the activities within this chapter so that you can perform a comparison of different models over the same dataset. Also, start this activity by using the preprocessed data that we prepared during the exploration of the dataset.
>
> The solution for this activity can be found on page 202.

Decision Tree Algorithm

The **decision tree algorithm** performs classifications based on a sequence that resembles a tree-like structure. It works by dividing the dataset into small subsets that serve as guides to develop the decision tree nodes. The nodes can be either decision nodes or leaf nodes, where the former represents a question or decision, and the latter represents the decisions made or the final outcome.

How Does It Work?

Considering this, decision trees continually split the dataset according to the parameters defined in the decision nodes. Decision nodes have branches coming out of them, where each decision node can have two or more branches. The branches represent the different possible answers that define the way in which the data is split.

Take, for instance, the following table, which shows whether a person has a pending student loan based on their age, highest education, and current income:

Age	Highest Education	Current Income	Target
25	Bachelor	0	Yes
32	Doctorate	120,000	Yes
48	Master	120,000	Yes
57	Master	150,000	No
29	College	50,000	No
35	Doctorate	230,000	No
69	Master	120,000	Yes
57	Doctorate	250,000	No
51	Bachelor	90,000	No
30	Master	115,000	Yes

Figure 4.7: Dataset for student loans

A possible configuration of a decision tree built based on the preceding data is shown in the following diagram, where the black boxes represent the decision nodes, the arrows are the branches representing each answer to the decision node, and the green boxes refer to the outcome for instances that follow the sequence:

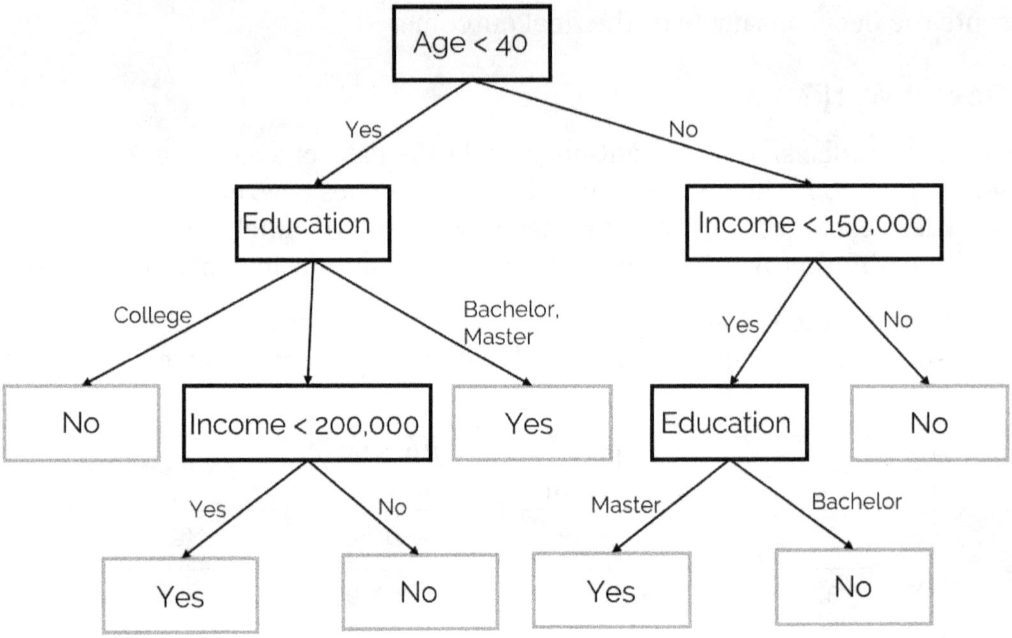

Figure 4.8: Decision tree constructed from data in Figure 4.7

To perform the prediction, once the decision tree is built, the model takes each instance and follows the sequence that matches the instance's features until it reaches a final leaf. According to this, the classification process starts at the root node (the one on top) and continues along the branch that describes the instance. This process continues until a leaf node is reached, which represents the prediction for that instance.

For instance, a person *over 40 years old*, with an income *below* $150,000, and an education level of *bachelor*, is likely to not have a student loan; hence, the class label assigned to it would be No.

Decision trees can handle both quantitative and qualitative features, considering that continuous features will be handled in ranges. Additionally, leaf nodes can handle categorical or continuous class labels; for categorical class labels, a classification is made, while for continuous class labels, the task to be handled is regression.

Exercise 16: Applying the Decision Tree Algorithm

In the following example, we will apply the Decision Tree algorithm to the Fertility Dataset, with the objective of determining whether the fertility level of an individual is affected by their demographics, their environmental conditions, and their previous medical conditions:

1. Open a Jupyter Notebook to implement this exercise.
2. Import **pandas** and read the **fertility_Diagnosis** dataset that you downloaded in *Exercise 15*. Make sure to add the argument **header** equal to **None** to the **read_csv** function, considering that the dataset does not contain a header row:

    ```
    import pandas as pd
    data = pd.read_csv("datasets/fertility_Diagnosis.csv", header=None)
    ```

3. Split the data into **X** and **Y**, considering that the class label is found under the column with index equal to 9. Use the following code:

    ```
    X = data.iloc[:,:9]
    Y = data.iloc[:,9]
    ```

4. Import scikit-learn's **DecisionTreeClassifier** class. Then, initialize it and use the **fit** function to train the model using **X** and **Y**:

    ```
    from sklearn.tree import DecisionTreeClassifier
    model = DecisionTreeClassifier()
    model.fit(X, Y)
    ```

    Again, an output from running this code snippet will appear. This output summarizes the conditions that define your model by printing the values used for every hyperparameter that the model uses.

    As the model has been initialized without setting any hyperparameters, the summary will show the default values used for each.

5. Finally, perform a prediction by using the model that you trained before, for the same instance as in *Exercise 15*: -0.33, 0.69, 0, 1, 1, 0, 0.8, 0, 0.88.

    Use the following code:

    ```
    pred = model.predict([[-0.33,0.69,0,1,1,0,0.8,0,0.88]])
    print(pred)
    ```

    Again, the model should predict the instance's class label as **N**.

Congratulations! You have successfully trained a Decision Tree model.

Activity 12: Training a Decision Tree Model for Our Census Income Dataset

You continue to work on building a model that's able to predict a person's annual income. Using the same dataset, you have chosen to build a Decision Tree model:

1. Open the Jupyter Notebook that you used for the previous activity.
2. Using the preprocessed Census Income Dataset that was previously split into different subsets, import the `DecisionTreeClassifier` class, and then use the `fit` method to train the model on the training sets (`X_train` and `Y_train`).
3. Finally, perform a prediction by using the model that you trained before for a new instance with the following values for each feature: 39, 6, 13, 4, 0, 2174, 0, 40, 38.

   The prediction for the individual should be equal to zero, meaning that the individual most likely has an income less than, or equal to 50K.

> **Note**
>
> The solution for this activity can be found on page 204.

Support Vector Machine Algorithm

The **support vector machine** (**SVM**) algorithm is a classifier that finds the hyperplane that effectively separates the observations into their class labels. It starts by positioning each instance into a data space with *n* dimensions, where n represents the number of features. Next, it traces an imaginary line that clearly separates the instances belonging to a class label from the instances belonging to others.

A support vector refers to the coordinates of a given instance. According to this, the support vector machine is the boundary that effectively segregates the different support vectors in a data space.

For a two-dimensional data space, the hyperplane is a line that splits the data space into two sections, each one representing a class label.

How Does It Work?

The following diagram shows a simple example of an SVM model. Both the green and orange dots represent the instances from the input dataset, where the colors define the class label to which each instance belongs. The dashed line signifies the hyperplane that clearly segregates the data points, which is defined based on the data points' location in data space. This line is used to classify unseen data, as represented by the grey dot. This way, new instances that are located to the left of the line will be classified as green, while the ones to the right will be orange.

The larger the number of features, the more dimensions the data space will have, which will make visual representation of the model difficult:

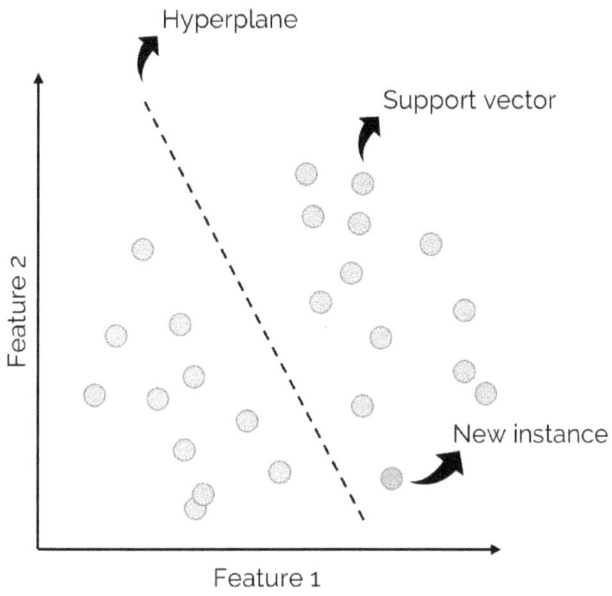

Figure 4.9: Graphical example of an SVM model

Although the algorithm seems to be quite simple, the complexity is evident in the algorithm's methodology for drawing the appropriate hyperplane. This is because the model generalizes to hundreds of observations with multiple features.

To choose the right hyperplane, the algorithm follows the following rules, wherein rule 1 is more important than rule 2, which in turn is more important than rule 3:

1. The hyperplane must maximize the correct classification of instances. This basically means that the best line is the one that effectively separates data points belonging to different class labels, while keeping those that belong to the same one together.

For instance, in the following diagram, although both lines are able to separate most instances into their correct class labels, line A would be selected by the model as the one that segregates the classes better than line B, which leaves one green instance among the orange ones:

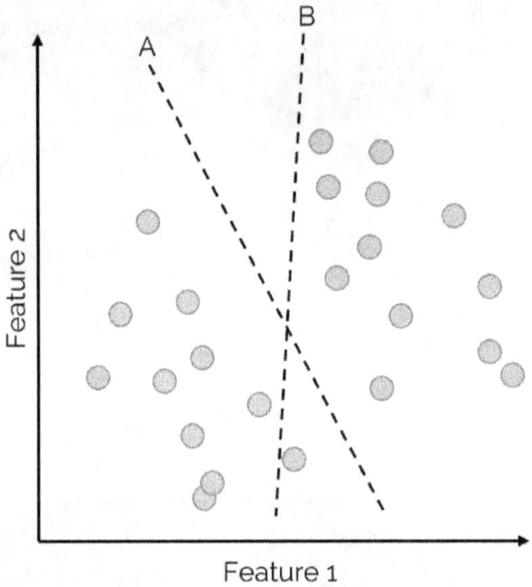

Figure 4.10: Sample of hyperplanes that explain rule 1

2. The hyperplane must maximize its distance to the nearest data point of either of the class labels, which is also known as the margin. This rule helps the model to become more robust, which means that the model is able to generalize the input data to also work efficiently over unseen data. This rule is especially important in preventing the mislabeling of new instances.

For example, by looking at the following diagram, it is possible to conclude that both hyperplanes comply with rule 1. Nevertheless, line A is selected, since it maximizes its distance to the nearest data points in comparison to the distance of line B to its nearest data point:

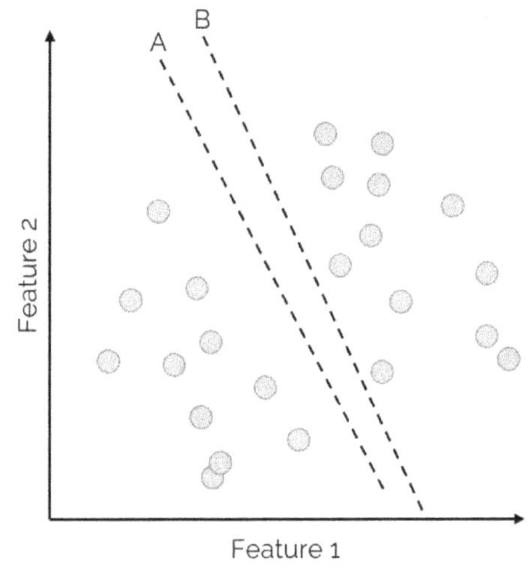

Figure 4.11: Sample of hyperplanes that explain rule 2

3. The final rule is used if the default configuration of the model is incapable of drawing a straight line to segregate classes. Take, for instance, the following diagram:

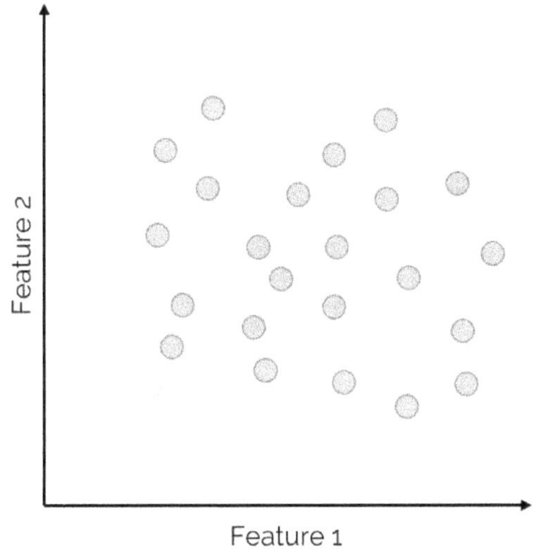

Figure 4.12: Sample observations that explain rule 3

To segregate these observations, the model will have to draw a circle or another similar shape. The algorithm handles this by using kernels that can add additional features that convert the distribution of data points into a form that allows a line to segregate them. There are several kernels available for this, and the selection of one should be done by trial and error, so that you can find the one that best handles the data that's available.

However, the default kernel to be used for the initial setup of an SVM model should be the **Radial Basis Function** (**RBF**) kernel. This is mainly because, based on several studies, this kernel has proved to work great for most data problems.

Exercise 17: Applying the SVM Algorithm

In this exercise, we will apply the SVM algorithm to the Fertility Dataset. The idea, which is the same as in previous exercises, is to determine whether the fertility level of an individual is affected by their demographics, their environmental conditions, and their previous medical conditions:

1. Open a Jupyter Notebook to implement this exercise.
2. Import **pandas** and read the **fertility_Diagnosis** dataset that you downloaded in *Exercise 15*. Make sure to add the argument **header = None** to the **read_csv** function, considering that the dataset does not contain a header row:

```
import pandas as pd
data = pd.read_csv("datasets/fertility_Diagnosis.csv", header=None)
```

3. Split the data into **X** and **Y**, considering that the class label is found under the column with index equal to 9. Use the following code:

```
X = data.iloc[:,:9]
Y = data.iloc[:,9]
```

4. Import scikit-learn's **SVC** class. Then, initialize it and use the **fit** function to train the model using **X** and **Y**:

```
from sklearn.svm import SVC
model = SVC()
model.fit(X, Y)
```

   Again, the output from running this code represents the summary of the model that was created. Additionally, a warning appears, stating that in future versions, the default values of some hyperparameters will change.

5. Finally, perform a prediction using the model that you trained previously, for the same instance as in *Exercise* 15: -0.33, 0.69, 0, 1, 1, 0, 0.8, 0, 0.88.

   Use the following code:

```
pred = model.predict([[-0.33,0.69,0,1,1,0,0.8,0,0.88]])
print(pred)
```

   Again, the model should predict the instance's class label as **N**.

Congratulations! You have successfully trained an SVM model.

Activity 13: Training an SVM Model for Our Census Income Dataset

Continuing with your task of building a model that is capable of predicting a person's annual income, the final algorithm that you want to train is the Support Vector Machine:

1. Open the Jupyter Notebook that you used for the previous activity.
2. Using the preprocessed Census Income Dataset that was previously split into different subsets, import the **SVC** class, and then use the **fit** method to train the model on the training sets (**X_train** and **Y_train**).

> **Note**
>
> The process of training the SVC class using the fit method may take a while.

3. Finally, perform a prediction using the model that you trained previously, for a new instance with the following values for each feature: 39, 6, 13, 4, 0, 2174, 0, 40, 38.

   The prediction for the individual should be equal to zero, that is, the individual most likely has an income less than or equal to 50K.

> **Note**
>
> Use the same Jupyter Notebook from the previous activity. Note that the dataset must have been preprocessed to obtain the desired results.
>
> The solution for this activity can be found on page 204.

Error Analysis

In the previous chapter, we explained the importance of error analysis. In this section, the different evaluation metrics will be calculated for all three models that were created in the previous activities, so that we can compare them.

Keep in mind that the selection of an evaluation metric is done according to the purpose of the case study. Nonetheless, next, we will compare the models using the accuracy, precision, and recall metrics, for learning purposes. This way, it will be possible to see that even though a model may be better in terms of one metric, it can be worse when measuring a different metric, which helps to emphasize the importance of choosing the right metric.

Accuracy, Precision, and Recall

As a quick reminder, in order to measure performance and perform error analysis, it is required that you use the **predict** method on the different sets of data (training, validation, and testing). The following code snippets present a clean way of measuring all three metrics on our three sets at once. The snippet is split into six bits of code, the purpose of which is explained as follows:

1. First, the three metrics to be used are imported:

```
from sklearn.metrics import accuracy_score, precision_score, recall_score
```

2. Next, we create two lists containing the names of the different sets of data that we will be using inside the **for** loop:

```
X_sets = [X_train, X_dev, X_test]
Y_sets = [Y_train, Y_dev, Y_test]
```

3. A dictionary will be created, which will hold the value of each evaluation metric for each set of data for each model:

```
metrics = {
"NB":{"Acc":[],"Pre":[],"Rec":[]},
"DT":{"Acc":[],"Pre":[],"Rec":[]},
"SVM":{"Acc":[],"Pre":[],"Rec":[]}
}
```

4. A **for** loop will be created, which will go from 0 to the length of the lists that were created in the first step. This is done to make sure that the prediction and the calculation of performance are performed over the three sets of data:

```
for i in range(0,len(X_sets)):

  pred_NB = model_NB.predict(X_sets[i])
```

```
metrics["NB"]["Acc"].append(accuracy_score(Y_sets[i], pred_NB))
metrics["NB"]["Pre"].append(precision_score(Y_sets[i], pred_NB))
metrics["NB"]["Rec"].append(recall_score(Y_sets[i], pred_NB))
```

The first line performs the prediction on a set of data, using the Naïve Bayes model that we built in previous chapters. Then, the calculation of all three metrics is done by comparing the ground truth data to the prediction that we calculated previously. The calculation is appended to the dictionary that was previously created.

5. We perform the same calculation as before, but use the Decision Tree model instead:

```
pred_tree = model_tree.predict(X_sets[i])
metrics["DT"]["Acc"].append(accuracy_score(Y_sets[i], pred_tree))
metrics["DT"]["Pre"].append(precision_score(Y_sets[i], pred_tree))
metrics["DT"]["Rec"].append(recall_score(Y_sets[i], pred_tree))
```

6. Again, we perform the same calculation using the SVM model:

```
pred_svm = model_svm.predict(X_sets[i])
metrics["SVM"]["Acc"].append(accuracy_score(Y_sets[i], pred_svm))
metrics["SVM"]["Pre"].append(precision_score(Y_sets[i], pred_svm))
metrics["SVM"]["Rec"].append(recall_score(Y_sets[i], pred_svm))
```

By using the preceding snippet, we get the following results:

		Naïve Bayes	Decision Tree	SVM
Accuracy	Training sets	0.7973	0.9778	0.9108
	Validation sets	0.7910	0.8140	0.8086
	Testing sets	0.8087	0.8286	0.8182
Precision	Training sets	0.6696	0.9875	0.8945
	Validation sets	0.6797	0.6313	0.7177
	Testing sets	0.6903	0.6332	0.7047
Recall	Training sets	0.3132	0.9198	0.7139
	Validation sets	0.2970	0.6009	0.3761
	Testing sets	0.3210	0.6287	0.3751

Figure 4.13: Performance results of all three models

Initially, the different inferences, in relation to selecting the best fitted model as well as with regard to the conditions that each model suffers from, will be done considering only the values from the accuracy metric, assuming a Bayes Error close to 0 (meaning that the model could reach a maximum success rate close to 1):

- Upon comparing the three accuracy scores of the Naïve Bayes model, it is possible to conclude that the model behaves almost the same way for all three datasets. This basically means that the model is generalizing the data from the training set, which allows it to perform well over unseen data. Nevertheless, the overall performance of the model is around 0.8, which is far from the maximum success rate.
- Moreover, the performance of both the Decision Tree and the SVM models, in terms of accuracy for the training set, is closer to the maximum success rate. However, both models are suffering from a case of overfitting, considering that the accuracy level of the models on the validation set is much lower than their performance on the training set. According to this, it would be possible to address the overfitting by adding more data into the training or by fine-tuning the hyperparameters of the model, which would help to bring up the accuracy level of the validation and testing sets.
- To choose the model that best fits the data, a comparison is done among the values obtained in the testing set, which, as explained in previous sections, is the one that determines the model's most likely overall performance on new data. Considering that all three models have similar accuracy levels on the testing set, it would be appropriate to address the issues related to the overfitting of the model by fine-tuning the hyperparameters in order to verify whether the accuracy on the testing set can be brought closer to 1.

Considering this, the researcher now has the required information to select a model and work on improving the results to achieve the maximum possible performance of the model.

Next, for learning purposes, let's compare the results of all the metrics for the Decision Tree model. Although the values for all three metrics prove the existence of overfitting, it is possible to observe that the degree of overfitting is much larger for the precision and recall metrics. Also, it is possible to conclude that the performance of the model on the training set measured by the recall metric is much lower, which means that the model is not as good at classifying positive labels. This means that if the purpose of the case study was to maximize the number of positive classifications, regardless of the classification of negative labels, the model needs to be greatly improved.

> **Note**
>
> The preceding comparison is done to show that the performance of the same model can vary if measured with a different metric. According to this, it is crucial to choose the metric of relevance for the case study.

Using the knowledge that you have gained from previous chapters, feel free to keep exploring the results shown in the preceding table.

Summary

Using the knowledge from previous chapters, we started this chapter by performing an analysis on the Census Income Dataset, with the objective of understanding the data available and making decisions for the preprocessing process. Three supervised learning classification algorithms–the Naïve Bayes algorithm, the Decision Tree algorithm, and the SVM algorithm–were explained, and were applied to the previously preprocessed dataset to create models that generalized to the training data. Finally, we compared the performance of the three models on the Census Income Dataset by calculating the accuracy, precision, and recall on the different sets of data (training, validation, and testing).

In the next chapter, we will look at Artificial Neural Networks (ANNs), their different types, and their advantages and disadvantages. We will also use the ANN to solve the same data problem that was discussed here, and to compare its performance with that of the other supervised learning algorithms.

5

Artificial Neural Networks: Predict Annual Income

Learning Objectives

By the end of this chapter, you will be able to:

- Explain the concept of neural networks
- Describe the processes of forward and backward propagation
- Solve a supervised learning classification problem using a neural network
- Analyze the results of the neural network by performing error analysis

This chapter explains the implementation of a Neural Network algorithm to a dataset in order to create a model that is able to predict future outcomes.

Introduction

In recent years, the field of artificial intelligence has focused on the concept of **artificial neural networks** (**ANNs**), also known as **Multilayer Perceptron**, mostly because they present a complex algorithm that can approach almost any challenging data problem. Even though the theory was developed decades back, during the 1940s, the networks are becoming more popular now, thanks to all the improvements in technology that allow for the gathering of large amounts of data as well as the developments in computer infrastructure that allow for the training of complex algorithms with large amounts of data.

Due to this, the following chapter will focus on introducing ANNs, their different types, and the advantages and disadvantages that they present. Additionally, an ANN will be used to solve the same data problem that was discussed in the previous chapter in order to present the differences in the performance of ANN in comparison to the other supervised learning algorithms.

Artificial Neural Networks

Although there are several machine learning algorithms available to solve data problems, as we have already stated, ANNs have become increasingly popular among data scientists, due to their capability to find patterns in large and complex datasets that cannot be interpreted by humans.

The **neural** part of the name refers to the resemblance of the architecture of the model to the anatomy of the human brain. This part is meant to replicate a human being's ability to learn from historical data by transferring bits of data from neuron to neuron until an outcome is reached.

In the following diagram, a human neuron is displayed, where A represents the **dendrites** that receive input information from other neurons, B refers to the **nucleus** of the neuron that processes the information, and C represents the **axon** that oversees the process of passing the processed information to the next neuron:

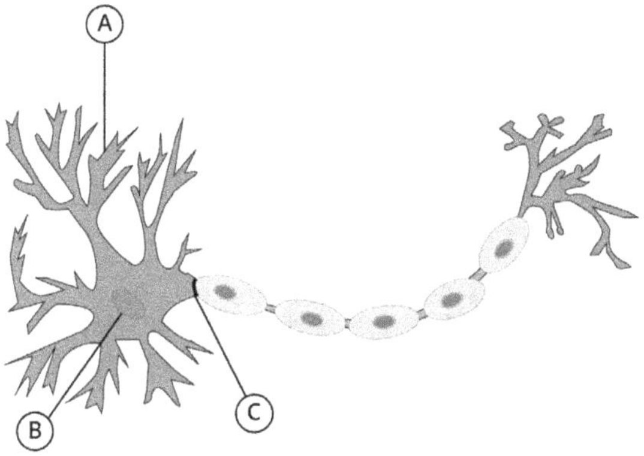

Figure 5.1: Visual representation of a human neuron

Moreover, the **artificial** part refers to the actual learning process of the model, where the main objective is to minimize the error in the model. It is an artificial learning process, considering that there is no real evidence regarding how human neurons process the information that they receive, and hence the model relies on mathematical functions that map an input to a desired output.

How Do They Work?

Before we dive into the process that is followed by an Artificial Neural Network, let's start by looking at its main components:

- **Input layer**: This layer is also known as `X`, as it contains all the data from the dataset (each instance with its features).
- **Hidden layers**: This layer is in charge of processing the input data in order to find patterns that are useful for making a prediction. The ANN can have as many hidden layers as desired, each with as many neurons (units) as required. The first layers are in charge of the simpler patterns, while the layers at the end search for the more complex ones.

  The hidden layers use a set of variables that represent weights and biases in order to help train the network. The values for the weights and biases are used as the variables that change in each iteration to approximate the prediction to the ground truth. This will be explained later.

- **Output layer**: Also known as **Y_hat**, this layer is the prediction made by the model, based on the data received from the hidden layers. This prediction is presented in the form of a probability, where the class label with a higher probability is the one selected as the prediction.

The following diagram illustrates the architecture of the preceding three layers:

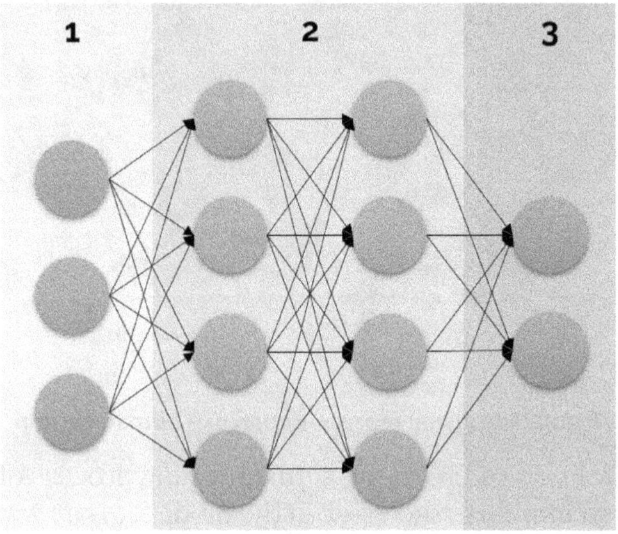

Figure 5.2: Basic architecture of an ANN

Take, as an analogy, a manufacturing process for building car parts. Here, the input layer consists of the raw materials, which in this case may be aluminum. The initial steps of the process involve polishing and cleaning the material, which can be seen as the first couple of hidden layers. Next, the material is bent to achieve the shape of the car part, which is handled by the deeper hidden layers. Finally, the part is delivered to the client, which can be considered to be the output layer.

Considering these steps, the main objective of the manufacturing process is to achieve a final part that highly resembles the part that the process aimed to build, meaning that the output, **Y_hat**, should maximize its similarity to **Y** (the ground truth) for a model to be considered a good fit to the data.

The actual methodology to train an ANN is an iterative process comprised of the following steps: forward propagation, calculation of the cost function, back-propagation, and weights and biases updates. Once the weights and biases are updated, the process starts again until the number of set iterations is met.

Let's explore each of the steps of the iteration process in detail.

Forward Propagation

The input layer feeds the initial information to the ANN. The processing of the data is done by propagating data bits through the depth (number of hidden layers) and width (number of units in each layer) of the network. The information is processed by each layer using a linear function, coupled with an activation function that aims to break the linearity, as follows:

$$Z_1 = W_1 * X + b_1$$

$$A_1 = \sigma(Z_1)$$

Figure 5.3: The linear and activation functions used by an ANN

Here, W_1 and b_1 are a matrix and a vector containing the weights and biases, respectively, and serve as the variables that can be updated through the iterations to train the model. Z_1 is the linear function for the first hidden layer, and A_1 is the outcome from the unit after applying an activation function (represented by the sigma symbol) to the linear one.

The preceding two formulas are calculated for each layer, where the value of X for the hidden layers (other than the first one) is replaced by the output of the previous layer (A_n), as follows:

$$Z_2 = W_2 * A_1 + b_2$$

$$A_2 = \sigma(Z_2)$$

Figure 5.4: The values calculated for the second layer of the ANN

Finally, the output from the last hidden layer is fed to the output layer, where the linear function is once again calculated, along with an activation function. The outcome from this layer is the one that will be compared to the ground truth in order to evaluate the performance of the algorithm before moving on to the next iteration.

The values of the weights for the first iteration are randomly initialized between 0 and 1, while the values for the biases can be set to 0 initially. Once the first iteration is run, the values will be updated, so that the process can start again.

The activation function can be of different types. Some of the most common ones are the **Rectified Linear Unit** (**ReLU**), the **Hyperbolic tangent** (**tanh**), the **Sigmoid**, and the **Softmax**.

Cost Function

Considering that the final objective of the training process is to build a model based on a given set of data, it is highly important to measure the model's ability to estimate a relation between **X** and **Y** by comparing the differences between the predicted value (**Y_hat**) and the ground truth (**Y**). This is accomplished by calculating the cost function (also known as the **loss function**) to determine how poor the model's predictions are. The cost function is calculated for each iteration to measure the progress of the model along the iteration process, with the objective of finding the values for the weights and biases that minimize the cost function.

For classification tasks, the cost function most commonly used is the **cross-entropy cost function**, where in the higher the value of the cost function, the greater the divergence between the predicted and actual values.

For a binary classification task, the cross-entropy cost function is calculated as follows:

$$cost = -(y * \log(y_{hat}) + (1 - y) * \log(1 - y_{hat}))$$

Figure 5.5: The cross-entropy cost function

Here, y would be either 1 or 0 (either of the two class labels), y_{hat} would be the probability calculated by the model, and *log* would be the natural logarithm.

For a multiclass classification task, the formula is as follows:

$$cost = -\sum_{c=1}^{M} y_c * \log(y_{hat,c})$$

Figure 5.6: The cost function for a multiclass classification task

Here, c represents a class label and M refers to the total number of class labels.

Once the cost function is calculated, the model proceeds and performs the back-propagation step, which will be explained in a moment.

Moreover, for regression tasks, the cost function would be the RMSE, which was explained in *Chapter 3, Supervised Learning: Key Steps.*

Back-Propagation

The back-propagation procedure was introduced as a part of the training process of ANNs to make learning faster. It basically involves calculating the partial derivatives of the cost function with respect to the weights and biases along the network. The objective of this is to minimize the cost function by changing the weights and the biases.

Considering that the weights and biases are not directly contained in the cost function, a chain rule is used to propagate the error from the cost function backwards until it reaches the first layers of the network. Next, a weighted average of the derivatives is calculated, which is used as the value to update the weights and biases before running a new iteration.

There are several algorithms that can be used to perform back-propagation, but the most common one is **gradient descent**. Gradient descent is an optimization algorithm that tries to find some local or global minimum of a function, which in this case is the cost function. It does so by determining the direction in which the model should move to reduce the error.

For instance, the following diagram displays an example of the training process of an ANN through the different iterations, where the job of back-propagation is to determine the direction in which the weights and biases should be updated, so that the error can continue to be minimized until it reaches a minimum point:

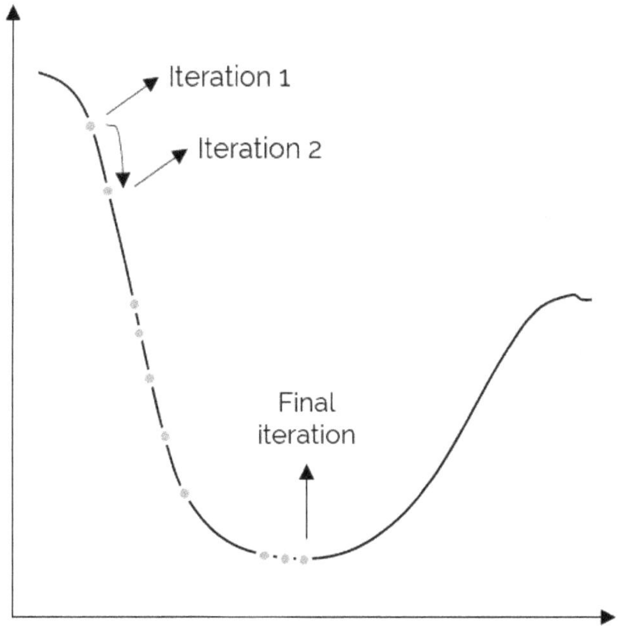

Figure 5.7: Example of the iterative process of training an ANN

It is important to highlight that back-propagation does not always find the global minima, since it stops updating once it has reached the lowest point in a slope, regardless of any other regions. Take, for instance, the following diagram:

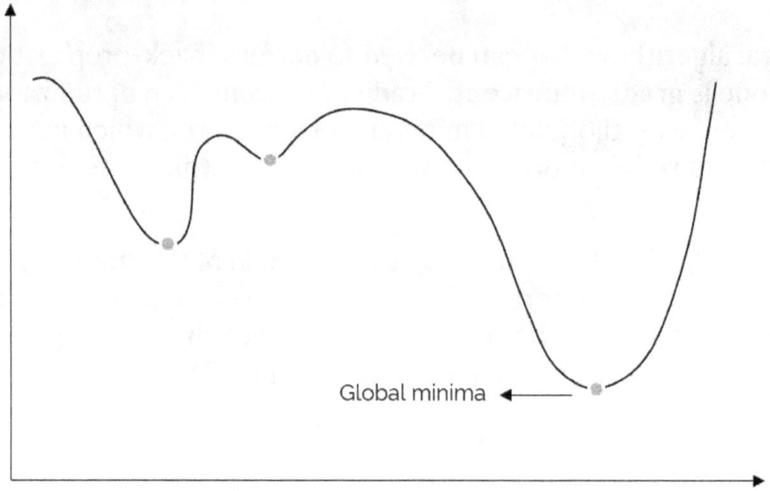

Figure 5.8: Examples of minimum points

Although all three points can be considered minimum points when compared to the points to their left and right, only one of them is the global minima.

Updating the Weights and Biases

Taking the derivatives' average that was calculated during back-propagation, the final step of an iteration is to update the values of the weights and biases. This process is done using the following formula:

$$New\ weight = old\ weight - derivative\ rate * learning\ rate$$

$$New\ bias = old\ bias - derivative\ rate * learning\ rate$$

Figure 5.9: Iterative formula for updating weights and biases

Here, the old values are those used to perform the forward propagation step, the derivative rate is the value obtained from the back-propagation step and is different for the weights and the biases, and the learning rate is a constant that is used to neutralize the effect of the derivative rate, so that the changes in the weights and biases are small and smooth. This has proven to help reach the lowest point more quickly.

Once the weights and the biases have been updated, the entire process starts again.

Understanding the Hyperparameters

Hyperparameters, as you have seen so far, are parameters that can be fine-tuned to improve the accuracy of a model. For neural networks, hyperparameters can be classified into two main groups: those that alter the structure of the network and those that modify the process to train it.

An important part of building an ANN is the process of fine-tuning the hyperparameters by performing error analysis and by playing around with the hyperparameters that help to solve the condition that is affecting the network. As a general reminder, networks suffering from high bias can usually be handled by creating bigger networks or training for longer durations of time, whereas networks suffering from high variance can benefit from the addition of more training data or by introducing a regularization technique.

Considering that the number of hyperparameters that can be changed for training an ANN is large, the most commonly used ones will be explained in the following sections.

Number of Hidden Layers and Units

The number of hidden layers and the number of units in each layer can be set by the researcher, as mentioned previously. Again, there is no exact science to selecting this number, and on the contrary, the selection of this number is a part of the fine-tuning process to test different approximations.

Nonetheless, when selecting the number of hidden layers, some data scientists lean toward an approach wherein multiple networks are trained, each with an extra layer. The model with the lowest error is the one with the right number of hidden layers. Unfortunately, this approach does not always work well, as more complex data problems do not really show a difference in performance through simply changing the number of hidden layers, regardless of the other hyperparameters.

On the other hand, there are several techniques that you can use to choose the number of units in a hidden layer. It is common for data scientists to choose the initial values for both of these hyperparameters based on similar research papers that are available online. This means that a good starting point would be copying the architecture of networks that have been successfully used for projects in a similar field, and then, through error analysis, fine-tuning the hyperparameters to improve performance.

Nonetheless, as per research activity, it is important to consider that deeper networks (networks with many hidden layers) outperform wider networks (networks with many units in each layer).

Activation Function

As mentioned previously, the activation function is used to introduce non-linearity to the model. The selection of an activation function should be done by considering that, conventionally, both the ReLU and the Hyperbolic tangent activation functions are used for all of the hidden layers, with ReLU being the most popular one among scientists.

On the other hand, the Sigmoid and the Softmax activation functions should be used for the output layer, as their outcome is in the form of a probability. Moreover, the Sigmoid activation function is used for binary classification problems, as it only outputs the probability for two class labels, whereas the Softmax activation function can be used for either binary or multiclass classification problems.

Regularization

Regularization is a technique used in machine learning to fix a model that is suffering from overfitting, which means that this hyperparameter is mostly used when it is strictly required, and its main objective is to increase the generalization ability of the model.

There are different regularization techniques, but the most common ones are the L1, L2, and dropout techniques. Although scikit-learn only supports L2 for its Multilayer Perceptron classifier, brief explanations of the three forms of regularization are as follows:

- The L1 and L2 techniques add a regularization term to the cost function as a way of penalizing high weights that may be affecting the performance of the model. The main difference between these approaches is that the regularization term for L1 is the absolute value of the magnitude of the weights, while for L2, it is the squared magnitude of the weights. For regular data problems, L2 has proven to work better, while L1 is mainly popular for feature extraction tasks since it creates sparse models.
- Dropout, on the other hand, refers to the model's ability to drop out some units in order to ignore their output during a step in the iteration, which simplifies the neural network. The dropout value is set between 0 and 1, and it represents the percentage of units that will be ignored. The units that are ignored are different in each iteration step.

Batch Size

Another hyperparameter to be tuned during the construction of an ANN is the batch size. This refers to the number of instances to be fed to the neural network during an iteration, which will be used to perform a forward and a backward pass through the network. For the next iteration, a new set of instances will be used.

This technique also helps to improve the model's ability to generalize to the training data because, in each iteration, it is fed with new combinations of instances, which is useful when dealing with an overfitted model.

> **Note**
>
> As per the result of many years of research, a good practice is to set the batch size to a value that is a multiple of 2. Some of the most common values are 32, 64, 128, and 256.

Learning Rate

The learning rate, as was explained previously, is introduced to help determine the size of the steps that the model will take to get to the local or global minima in each iteration. The lower the learning rate, the slower the learning process of the network, but this results in better models. On the other hand, the larger the learning rate, the faster the learning process of the model; however, this may result in a model not converging.

> **Note**
>
> The default learning rate value is usually set to 0.001.

Number of Iterations

A neural network is trained through an iterative process, as was mentioned previously. Therefore, it is necessary to set the number of iterations that the model will perform. The best way to set up the ideal number of iterations is to start low, between 200 and 500, and increase it, in the event that the plot of the cost function over each iteration shows a decreasing line. Needless to say, the larger the number of iterations, the longer it takes to train a model.

Additionally, increasing the number of iterations is a technique known to address underfitted networks. This is because it gives the network more time to find the right weights and biases that generalize to the training data.

Applications

In addition to the preceding architecture, a number of new architectures have emerged over time, thanks to the popularity of neural networks. Some of the most popular ones are **convolutional neural networks**, which can handle the processing of images by using filters as layers, and **recurrent neural networks**, which are used to process sequences of data such as text translations.

Due to this, the applications of neural networks extend to almost any data problem, ranging from simple to complex. While a neural network is capable of finding patterns in really large datasets (either for classification or regression tasks), they are also known for effectively handling challenging problems, such as the creation of self-driving cars, the construction of chatbots, the recognition of faces, and so on.

Limitations

Some of the limitations of training neural networks are as follows:

- The training process takes time. Regardless of the hyperparameters used, they generally take time to converge.
- They need very large datasets in order to work better. Neural networks are meant for larger datasets, as their main advantage is their ability to find patterns within millions of values.
- They are considered a black box as there is no actual knowledge of how the network arrives at a result. Although the math behind the training process is clear, it is not possible to know what assumptions the model makes while being trained.
- The hardware requirements are large. Again, the greater the complexity of the problem, the larger the hardware requirements.

Although ANNs can be applied to almost any data problem, due to their limitations, it is always a good practice to test other algorithms when dealing with simpler data problems. This is important because applying neural networks to data problems that can be solved by simpler models makes the costs outweigh the benefits.

Applying an Artificial Neural Network

Now that you know the components of an artificial neural network as well as the different steps that it follows to train a model and make predictions, let's train a simple network using the scikit-learn library.

In this topic, scikit-learn's neural network module will be used to train a network using the dataset from the previous chapter (the Census Income Dataset). It is important to mention that scikit-learn is not the most appropriate library for neural networks, as it does not currently support many types of neural networks, and its performance over deeper networks is not as good as other neural network specialized libraries, such as TensorFlow.

The neural network module in scikit-learn currently supports a Multilayer Perceptron for classification, a Multilayer Perceptron for regression, and a Restricted Boltzmann Machine architecture. Considering that the case study consists of a classification task, the Multilayer Perceptron for classifications will be used.

Scikit-Learn's Multilayer Perceptron

A **Multilayer Perceptron** (**MLP**) is a supervised learning algorithm that, as its name indicates, uses multiple layers (hidden layers) to learn a non-linear function that translates the input values into output, either for classification or regression. As we explained previously, the job of each unit of a layer is to transform the data received from the previous layer by calculating a linear function and then applying an activation function to break the linearity.

It is important to mention that an MLP has a non-convex loss function which, as mentioned previously, signifies that there may be multiple local minima. This means that different initializations of the weights and biases will result in different trained models, which in turn indicates different accuracy levels.

The Multilayer Perceptron classifier in scikit-learn has around 20 different hyperparameters associated with the architecture or the learning process, which can be altered in order to modify the training process of the network. Fortunately, all of these hyperparameters have set default values, which allows us to run a first model without much effort. The results from this model can then be used to tune the hyperparameters as required.

To train an MLP classifier, it is required that you input two arrays: first, the `X` input of dimensions (`n_samples`, `n_features`) containing the training data, and then the `Y` input of dimensions (`n_sample`,) that contains the label values for each sample.

Similar to the algorithms that we looked at in the previous chapter, the model is trained using the **fit** method, and then predictions can be achieved by using the **predict** method on the trained model.

Exercise 18: Applying the Multilayer Perceptron Classifier Class

In this exercise, you will learn how to train a scikit-learn's Multilayer Perceptron to solve a classification task:

> **Note**
>
> For the exercises and activities within this chapter, you will need to have Python 3.6, NumPy, Jupyter, Pandas, and scikit-learn installed on your system.

1. Open a Jupyter Notebook to implement this exercise.
2. Using the Fertility Dataset from the previous chapter, import **pandas** and read the **.csv** file. Make sure that you add the argument **header** equal to **None** to the **read_csv** function, considering that the dataset does not contain a header row:

```
import pandas as pd
data = pd.read_csv("datasets/fertility_Diagnosis.csv", header=None)
```

3. Split the dataset into **X** and **Y** sets in order to separate the features data from the label values:

```
X = data.iloc[:,:9]
Y = data.iloc[:,9]
```

4. Import the **MLPClassifier** class from the **neural_network** module and use the **fit** method to train a model. When initializing the model, leave all the hyperparameters at their default values, but add a **random_state** equal to 101 to ensure that you get the same results as the one shown in this exercise:

```
from sklearn.neural_network import MLPClassifier
model = MLPClassifier(random_state=101)
model = model.fit(X, Y)
```

5. Address the warning that appears after running the **fit** method:

```
/home/daniel/Desktop/VirtualEnvs/explore_data/lib/python3.6/site-packages/sklearn/neural_network/multilayer_perceptron.p
y:562: ConvergenceWarning: Stochastic Optimizer: Maximum iterations (200) reached and the optimization hasn't converged
yet.
  % self.max_iter, ConvergenceWarning)
```

Figure 5.10: Warning message displayed after running the fit method

As you can see, the warning specifies that after running the default number of iterations, which is 200, the model has not reached convergence. To address this issue, try higher values for the iterations, until the warning stops appearing. To change the number of iterations, add the **max_iter = Desired number** argument inside of the parentheses during the initialization of the model:

```
model = MLPClassifier(random_state=101, max_iter =1200)
model = model.fit(X, Y)
```

Further more, the output below the warning explains the values used for all of the hyperparameters of the Multilayer Perceptron.

6. Finally, perform a prediction by using the model that you trained previously, for a new instance with the following values for each feature: −0.33, 0.69, 0, 1, 1, 0, 0.8, 0, 0.88.

   Use the following code:

```
pred = model.predict([[-0.33,0.69,0,1,1,0,0.8,0,0.88]])
print(pred)
```

   The model's prediction is equal to **N**, that is, the model predicts the person with the specified features to have a normal diagnosis.

Congratulations! You have successfully trained a Multilayer Perceptron model.

Activity 14: Training a Multilayer Perceptron for Our Census Income Dataset

With the objective of comparing the performance of the algorithms trained in the previous chapter with the performance of a neural network, for this activity, we will continue to work with the Census Income Dataset that we downloaded previously. Consider the following scenario: your company is continually offering a book for employees to improve their abilities, and you have recently learned about neural networks and their power. You have decided to build a network to model the dataset that you were given previously in order to test whether a neural network is better at predicting a person's income based on their demographical data.

> **Note**
>
> Start this activity using the preprocessed data from the previous chapter (Census Income Dataset). This means that all the irrelevant features must have been deleted and quantitative features must have been converted into their numeric forms. Otherwise, the results from the activity may vary from the ones presented in the solution section.

Follow these steps to complete this activity:

1. Using the preprocessed Census Income Dataset, separate the features from the target, creating the variables **X** and **Y**.
2. Divide the dataset into training, validation, and testing sets, using a split ratio of 10%.

> **Note**
>
> Remember to continue using a **random_state** equal to 101 when performing the dataset split in order to set a seed to ensure the same results in every run of the code.

3. From the **neural_network** module, import the Multilayer Perceptron Classifier class. Initialize it and train the model with the training data.

   Leave all the hyperparameters at their default values. Again, use a **random_state** equal to 101.
4. Address any warning that may appear after training the model with the default values for the hyperparameters.
5. Calculate the accuracy of the model for all three sets (training, validation, and testing).

> **Note**
>
> The solution for this activity can be found on page 206.

The accuracy score for the three sets should be as follows:

Train sets = 0.8342

Dev sets = 0.8111

Test sets = 0.8252

Performance Analysis

In the following section, we will first perform error analysis using the accuracy metric as a tool to determine the condition that is affecting the performance of the algorithm in greater proportion. Once the model is diagnosed, the hyperparameters can be tuned to improve the overall performance of the algorithm. The final model will be compared to those that were created during the previous chapter in order to determine whether a neural network outperforms the other models.

Error Analysis

Using the accuracy score calculated in *Activity* 14, we can calculate the error rates for each of the sets and compare them against each other to diagnose the condition that is affecting the model. To do so, a Bayes Error equal to 1% will be assumed, considering that other models in the previous chapter were able to achieve an accuracy level over 97%:

	Accuracy score	Error rate	Difference
Bayes Error		0.01	
Training sets	0.8342	0.1658	0.1558
Validation sets	0.8111	0.1889	0.0231
Testing sets	0.8252	0.1748	-0.0141

Figure 5.11: Accuracy score and error rate of the network

> **Note**
>
> Remember that in order to detect the condition that is affecting the network, it is necessary to take an error rate and subtract from it the value of the error rate above it. The biggest positive difference is the one that we use to diagnose the model.

According to the column of differences, it is evident that the biggest difference is found between the error rate in the training set and the Bayes Error. Based on this, it is possible to conclude that the model is suffering from *high bias*, which, as explained in previous chapters, can be handled by training a bigger network for longer periods of time (a higher number of iterations).

Hyperparameter Fine-Tuning

Through error analysis, it was possible to determine that the network is suffering from high bias. This is highly important, as it indicates the actions that need to be taken in order to improve the performance of the model in greater proportion.

Considering that both the number of iterations and the size of the network (number of layers and units) should be changed using a trial-and-error approach, the following experiments will be done:

	Default values	Experiment 1	Experiment 2	Experiment 3
Number of iterations	200	500	500	500
Number of hidden layers	1	1	2	3
Number of units per layer	100	100	100,100	100,100,100

Figure 5.12: Suggested experiments to tune the hyperparameters

> **Note**
>
> Some experiments may take longer to run due to their complexity. For instance, Experiment 3 will take longer than Experiment 2.

The idea behind these experiments is to be able to test different values in order to find out whether an improvement can be achieved. If the improvements achieved through these experiments are significant, further experiments should be considered.

Similar to adding the `random_state` argument to the initialization of the Multilayer Perceptron, the change in the values of the number of iterations and the size of the network can be achieved, using the following code, which shows the values for Experiment 3:

```
from sklearn.neural_network import MLPClassifier

model = MLPClassifier(random_state=101, max_iter = 500, hidden_layer_
sizes=(100,100,100))

model = model.fit(X_train, Y_train)
```

> **Note**
>
> To find what term to use to change each hyperparameter, visit scikit-learn's MLPClassifier page at: http://scikit-learn.org/stable/modules/generated/sklearn.neural_network.MLPClassifier.html.

As you can see in the preceding snippet, the **max_iter** argument is used to set the number of iterations to run during the training of the network. On the other hand, the **hidden_layer_sizes** argument is used to both set the number of hidden layers and set the number of units in each. For instance, in the preceding example, by setting the argument to (100,100,100), the architecture of the network is of three hidden layers, each with 100 units. Of course, this architecture also includes the required input and output layers.

The accuracy scores from running the preceding experiments can be seen in the following table:

	Initial model	Experiment 1	Experiment 2	Experiment 3
Training sets	0.8342	0.8342	0.8406	0.8297
Validation sets	0.8111	0.8111	0.8166	0.8043
Testing sets	0.8252	0.8252	0.8375	0.8231

Figure 5.13: Accuracy scores for all experiments

> **Note**
>
> Keep in mind that the main purpose behind tuning the hyperparameters is to decrease the difference between the error rate of the training set and the Bayes Error, which is why most of the analysis is done by considering only this value.

Through an analysis of the accuracy scores of the experiments, it can be concluded that the best configuration of hyperparameters is the one used during Experiment 2. Additionally, it is possible to conclude that there is most likely no point in trying other values for the number of iterations or the number of hidden layers, considering that increasing the number of iterations did not have an effect on the performance of the algorithm and adding three hidden layers decreased the performance of the network.

Nonetheless, in order to test the width of the hidden layers, the following experiments will be considered, using the selected values for the number of iterations and the number of hidden layers, but varying the number of units in each layer:

	Initial model (Experiment 2)	Experiment 1	Experiment 2	Experiment 3	Experiment 4
Number of iterations	500	500	500	500	500
Number of hidden layers	2	2	2	2	2
Number of units per layer	100,100	50,50	150,150	25,25	175,175

Figure 5.14: Suggested experiments to vary the width of the network

Here, the first two experiments were thought up in advance, while the other two were designed after finding out the performance of the previous ones. Next, the accuracy score of all four experiments is shown, followed by an explanation of the logic behind them:

	Initial model (Experiment 2)	Experiment 1	Experiment 2	Experiment 3	Experiment 4
Training sets	0.8406	0.8412	0.8508	0.8159	0.8807
Validation sets	0.8166	0.8191	0.8289	0.8022	0.8375
Testing sets	0.8375	0.8391	0.8504	0.8225	0.8483

Figure 5.15: Accuracy scores for the second round of experiments

Although the accuracy improved for the first two experiments, it was found that using 150 units per layer achieved better results. Experiment 3 then tested whether a smaller number of units per layer would continue to improve results, which was not the case. Additionally, Experiment 4 tested with a higher number of units, which returned higher results for both the training and validation sets, but not for the testing set.

By observing these values, it can be concluded that the performance of experiment 2 is the highest in terms of testing sets, which leaves us with a network that iterates for 500 steps, with one input and output layer and two hidden layers with 150 units each.

> **Note**
>
> There is no ideal way to test the different configurations of hyperparameters. The only important thing to consider is that the focus is centered on those hyperparameters that solve the condition that is affecting the network in a greater proportion. Feel free to try more experiments if you wish.

Considering the accuracy scores of all three sets of Experiment 2 to calculate the error rate, the biggest difference is still between the training set error and the Bayes Error. This means that the model may not be the best fit for the dataset, considering that the training set error could not be brought closer to the minimum possible error margin.

Model Comparison

When more than one model has been trained, the final step related to the process of creating a model is a comparison between the models in order to choose the one that best represents the training data in a generalized way, so that it works well over unseen data.

The comparison, as mentioned previously, must be done by using only the metric that was selected to measure the performance of the models for the data problem. This is important, considering that one model can perform very differently for each metric, so the model that maximizes the performance with the ideal metric should be selected.

Although the metric is calculated on all three sets of data (training, validation, and testing) in order to be able to perform error analysis, for most cases, the comparison and selection should be done by prioritizing the results obtained with the testing set. This is mainly due to the purpose of the sets, considering that the training set is used to create the model, the validation set is used to fine-tune the hyperparameters, and finally, the testing set is used to measure the overall performance of the model on unseen data.

Taking this into account, the model with a higher performance on the testing set, after having improved all models to their fullest potential, will be the one that performs best on unseen data.

Activity 15: Comparing Different Models to Choose the Best Fit for the Census Income Data Problem

Consider the following scenario: after training four different models with the available data, you have been asked to perform an analysis to choose the model that best suits the case study.

> **Note**
>
> The following activity is mainly analytical. Use the results obtained from the activities in the previous chapter, as well as the activity in the current chapter.

Follow these steps to compare the different models:

1. Open the Jupyter Notebook that you used to train the models.
2. Compare the four models, based only on their accuracy scores. Fill in the details in the following table:

	Naïve Bayes	Decision Tree	SVM	Multilayer Perceptron
Training sets				
Validation sets				
Testing sets				

Figure 5.16: Accuracy scores of all four models for the Census Income Dataset

On the basis of the accuracy scores, identify the model with the best performance.

> **Note**
>
> The solution for this activity can be found on page 207.

Summary

This chapter mainly focused on artificial neural networks (the Multilayer Perceptron, in particular), which have become increasingly important in the field of machine learning due to their capability to tackle highly complex data problems that usually use extremely large datasets with patterns that are impossible to look at by the human eye.

The main objective is to emulate the architecture of the human brain by using mathematical functions to process data.

The process that is used to train an ANN consists of a forward propagation process, the calculation of a cost function, a back-propagation process, and the update of the different weights and biases that help to map the input values to an output.

In addition to the variables of the weights and biases, ANNs have multiple hyperparameters that can be tuned to improve the performance of the network, which can be done by modifying the architecture or training process of the algorithm. Some of the most popular hyperparameters are the size of the network (in terms of hidden layers and units), the number of iterations, the regularization term, the batch size, and the learning rate.

Once these concepts were covered, we created a simple network to tackle the Census Income Dataset problem that was introduced in the previous chapter. Next, by performing error analysis, we fine tuned some of the hyperparameters of the network to improve its performance.

6

Building Your Own Program

Learning Objectives

By the end of this chapter, you will be able to:

- Explain the key stages involved in building a comprehensive program
- Save a model in order to get the same results every time it is run
- Call a saved model to use it for predictions on unseen data
- Create an interactive version of your program so that anyone can use it effectively

This chapters presents all the steps required to solve a problem using machine learning.

Introduction

In the previous chapters, we covered the main concepts of machine learning, beginning with the distinction between the two main learning approaches (supervised and unsupervised learning), and moving on to the specifics of some of the most popular algorithms in the data scientist community.

This chapter will talk about the importance of building complete machine learning programs, rather than just training models. This will involve taking the models to the next level, where they can be accessed and used easily.

This is especially important when working in a team, either for a company or for research purposes, as it allows all members of the team to use the model without fully understanding it.

Program Definition

The following section will cover the key stages required to construct a comprehensive machine learning program that allows easy access to the trained model in order to perform predictions for all future data. These stages will be applied to the construction of a program that allows for a bank to determine the promotional strategy for a financial product in their marketing campaign.

Building a Program: Key Stages

At this point, you should be able to preprocess a dataset, build different models using training data, and compare those models, in order to choose the one that best fits the data at hand. These are some of the processes handled during the first two stages of building a program, which ultimately allow for the creation of the model. Nonetheless, a program should also consider the process of saving the final model, as well as the ability to perform quick predictions without the need for coding.

The processes that we just discussed are divided into three main stages, and will be explained in the following sections. These stages represent the foremost requirements of any machine learning project.

Preparation

Preparation consists of all the procedures that we've developed thus far, with the objective of outlining the project in alignment with the available information and the desired outcome. The following is a brief description of the three processes in this stage (these have been discussed in detail in previous chapters):

1. *Data Exploration*: Once the objective of the study has been established, data exploration is undertaken in order to understand the data that is available and to obtain valuable insights. These insights will be used later to make decisions regarding the preprocessing and division of the data and the selection of models, among other uses. The information most commonly obtained during data exploration includes the size of the data (number of instances and features), the irrelevant features, and whether missing values or evident outliers are present.
2. *Data Preprocessing*: As we have discussed, data preprocessing primarily refers to the process of handling missing values, outliers, and noisy data; converting qualitative features into their numeric forms; and normalizing or standardizing these values. This process can be done manually in any data editor such as Excel, or by using libraries to code the procedure.
3. *Data Splitting*: The final process, data splitting, involves splitting the entire dataset into two or three sets (depending on the approach) that will be used for training, validating, and testing the overall performance of the model. The separation of the features and the class label is also handled during this stage.

Creation

This stage involves all of the steps that are required to create a model that fits the data that is available. This can be done by selecting different algorithms, training and tuning them, comparing the performance of each, and finally, selecting the one that generalizes best to the data (meaning that it achieves a better overall performance). The processes in this stage will be discussed briefly, as follows:

1. *Algorithm Selection*: Irrespective of whether you decide to choose one or multiple algorithms, it is crucial to select an algorithm on the basis of the available data and to take into consideration the advantages of each algorithm. This is important since many data scientists make the mistake of choosing neural networks for any data problem, when in reality, simpler problems can be tackled using simpler models that run more quickly and perform better with smaller datasets.
2. *Training Process*: This process involves training the model using the training set data. This means that the algorithm uses the features data (`X`) and the label classes (`Y`) to determine relationship patterns that will help generalize to unseen data and predict when the class label is not available.

3. *Model Evaluation*: This process is handled by measuring the performance of the algorithm through the metric selected for the study. As mentioned previously, it is important to choose the metric that best represents the purpose of the study, considering that the same model can do very well in terms of one metric and poorly in terms of another.

   While evaluating the model on the validation set, hyperparameters are fine-tuned to achieve the best possible performance. Once the hyperparameters have been tuned, the evaluation is performed on the testing set to measure the overall performance of the model on unseen data.

4. *Model Comparison and Selection*: When multiple models are created based on different algorithms, a model comparison is performed to select the one that outperforms the others. This comparison should be done by using the same metric for all the models.

Interaction

The final stage in building a comprehensive machine learning program consists of allowing the final user to easily interact with the model. This includes the process of saving the model into a file, the ability of calling the file that holds the saved model, and the development of a channel through which users can interact with the model:

1. *Storing the Final Model*: This process is introduced during the development of a machine learning program as it is crucial to enable the unaltered use of the model for future predictions. The process of saving the model is crucial, considering that most algorithms are randomly initialized each time they are run, which makes the results different for each run. The process of saving the model will be explained further later in this chapter.

2. *Loading the Model*: Once the model has been saved to a file, it can be accessed by loading the file into any code. The model is then stored in a variable that can be used to apply the `prediction` method on unseen data. This process will also be explained later in this chapter.

3. *Channel of Interaction*: Finally, it is crucial to develop an interactive and easy way to perform predictions using the saved model, especially because on many occasions, models are created by the technology team for other teams to use. This means that an ideal program should allow non-experts to use the model for prediction by simply typing in the required information. This idea will also be expanded upon later in this chapter.

The following diagram illustrates the preceding processes:

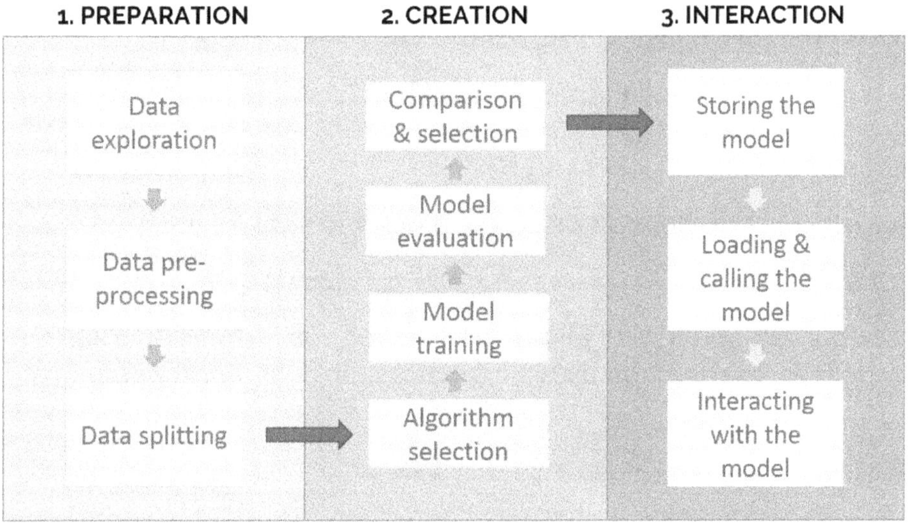

Figure 6.1: Stages for building a machine learning program

The rest of this chapter will focus on the final stage of building a model, considering that all the previous steps were discussed in previous chapters.

Understanding the Dataset

To learn how to implement the processes in the *Interaction* section, we will build a program that's capable of predicting whether a person will be interested in acquiring a specific product from the bank, which will help the bank to target its promotion efforts. The dataset used to build this program is available at the UC Irvine Machine Learning Repository under the name **Bank Marketing Dataset**.

> **Note**
>
> To download this dataset, visit the following link: http://archive.ics.uci.edu/ml/datasets/Bank+Marketing.

Once you have located the repository, follow these steps to download the dataset:

1. First, click on the **Data Folder** link.
2. Download the **bank** folder.
3. Open the **.zip** folder and extract the **bank-full.csv** file.

To explore the dataset, follow these steps:

1. Open a Jupyter Notebook and load the dataset to explore it:

```
data = pd.read_csv("../datasets/bank-full.csv")
```

This file shows the values of all the features for one instance in a single column, since the **read_csv** function uses a comma as the delimiter for columns:

	age;"job";"marital";"education";"default";"balance";"housing";"loan";"contact";"day";"month";"duration";"campaign";"pdays";"previous";"poutcome";"y"
0	58;"management";"married";"tertiary";"no";2143...
1	44;"technician";"single";"secondary";"no";29;"...
2	33;"entrepreneur";"married";"secondary";"no";2...
3	47;"blue-collar";"married";"unknown";"no";1506...
4	33;"unknown";"single";"unknown";"no";1;"no";"n...

Figure 6.2: Screenshot of data in the .csv file before splitting the data into columns

2. To fix this, add the delimiter parameter to the **read_csv** function by using a semicolon as the delimiter, as shown in the following code snippet:

```
data = pd.read_csv("../datasets/bank-full.csv", delimiter = ";")
```

After this step, the file should look as follows:

	age	job	marital	education	default	balance	housing	loan	contact	day	month	duration	campaign	pdays	previous	poutcome	y
0	58	management	married	tertiary	no	2143	yes	no	unknown	5	may	261	1	-1	0	unknown	no
1	44	technician	single	secondary	no	29	yes	no	unknown	5	may	151	1	-1	0	unknown	no
2	33	entrepreneur	married	secondary	no	2	yes	yes	unknown	5	may	76	1	-1	0	unknown	no
3	47	blue-collar	married	unknown	no	1506	yes	no	unknown	5	may	92	1	-1	0	unknown	no
4	33	unknown	single	unknown	no	1	no	no	unknown	5	may	198	1	-1	0	unknown	no

Figure 6.3: Screenshot of data in the .csv file after splitting it into columns

As you can see in the preceding table, the file contains unknown values that should be handled as missing values.

3. To do so, let's replace the unknown string for **NaN** by using Numpy, as follows:

```
import numpy as np
data[data == "unknown"] = np.nan
```

Finally, the edited dataset is saved in a new **.csv** file, so that it can be used for the activities throughout this chapter. You can do this by using the **to_csv** function, as follows:

```
data.to_csv("../datasets/bank-full-dataset.csv")
```

The file should contain a total of 45,211 instances, each with 16 features and 1 class label. The class label is binary, of the type **yes** or **no**, and indicates whether the client subscribes to a term deposit with the bank.

Each instance represents a client of the bank, and the features capture demographic information, as well as data regarding the nature of the contact with the client during the current (and previous) promotional campaign.

The following table displays brief descriptions of all 16 features. This will help to determine the relevance of each feature to the study, and will provide an idea of some of the steps required to preprocess the data:

Name	Type	Description
age	Quantitative (continuous)	The age of the individual.
job	Qualitative (nominal)	The type of job the individual currently has. For instance: "blue-collar".
marital	Qualitative (nominal)	The marital status of the individual.
education	Qualitative (ordinal)	The highest education level achieved by the individual.
default	Qualitative (nominal - binary)	Whether the individual has credit by default.
balance	Quantitative (continuous)	Average yearly balance of the individual in euros.
housing	Qualitative (nominal - binary)	Whether the individual has any housing loan.
loan	Qualitative (nominal - binary)	Whether the individual has any personal loan.
contact	Qualitative (nominal)	The mode of communication used to contact the individual for the current campaign.
day	Quantitative (discrete)	The day of the month when the individual was last contacted for the current campaign.
month	Qualitative (nominal)	The month of the year when the individual was last contacted for the current campaign.
duration	Quantitative (continuous)	The duration, in seconds, of the last contact with the individual for the current campaign.
campaign	Quantitative (continuous)	The number of times the individual was contacted during the promotion campaign.
pdays	Quantitative (continuous)	The number of days that passed by after the individual was contacted for a previous campaign. The value -1 means that the client was not contacted for a previous campaign.
previous	Quantitative (continuous)	The number of times the individual was contacted for previous campaigns.
poutcome	Qualitative (nominal)	The outcome obtained from the previous campaign.

Figure 6.4: A table describing the features of the dataset

> Note
>
> You can find the preceding descriptions and more in the `.zip` folder, under the file named **`bank-names.txt`**.

Using the information obtained during the exploration of the dataset, it is possible to proceed with preprocessing the data and training the model, which will be the purpose of the following activity.

Activity 16: Performing the Preparation and Creation Stages for the Bank Marketing Dataset

The objective of this activity is to perform the processes in the preparation and creation stages to build a comprehensive machine learning problem.

> **Note**
>
> For the exercises and activities within this chapter, you will need to have Python 3.6, NumPy, Jupyter, Pandas, and scikit-learn installed on your system.

Let's consider the following scenario: you work at the principal bank in your town and the marketing team has decided that they want to know in advance if a client is likely to subscribe to a term deposit, in order to focus their efforts on targeting those clients. For this, you have been provided with a dataset containing details on current and previous marketing activities carried out by the team (the Bank Marketing Dataset that you downloaded and explored previously will be used). Your boss has asked you to preprocess the dataset and compare two models against each other, so that you can select the best one. Follow the steps given below to achieve this:

1. Open a Jupyter Notebook to implement this activity and import `pandas`.
2. Load the dataset into the notebook. Make sure that you load the one that was edited previously, named `bank-full-dataset.csv`.
3. Select the metric that is most appropriate for measuring the performance of the model, considering that the purpose of the study is to detect clients who are likely to subscribe to the term deposit.

4. Preprocess the dataset.

   Note that one of the qualitative features is ordinal, which is why it must be converted to a numeric form that follows the order. Use the following code snippet to do so:

```
data["education"] = data["education"].fillna["unknown"]
encoder = ["unknown", "primary", "secondary", "tertiary"]

for i, word in enumerate(encoder):
  data["education"] = data["education"].str.replace(word,str(i))
  data["education"] = data["education"].astype("int64")
```

5. Separate the features from the class label and split the dataset into three sets (training, validation, and testing).
6. Use the Decision Tree and the Multilayer Perceptron algorithms to apply to the dataset and train the models.

> **Note**
>
> You can also try this with the other classification algorithms discussed in this book. However, these two are mainly chosen so that you are also able to compare the difference in training times.

7. Evaluate both models by using the metric that you selected previously.
8. Fine-tune some of the hyperparameters to fix the issues detected during the evaluation of the model, by performing error analysis.
9. Compare the final versions of your models and select the one that you believe best fits the data.

> **Note**
>
> Do not use a **`random_state`** value to train the models. This is mainly because in subsequent activities, we will run the selected model several times to see the different results that can be achieved through different initializations.
>
> You can find the solution for this activity on page 209.

Saving and Loading a Trained Model

Although the process of manipulating a dataset and training the right model is crucial for developing a machine learning project, the work does not end there. Knowing how to save a trained model is key, as this will allow you to save the hyperparameters used and the initialized values for the different variables of your final model, so that it remains unchanged when it is run again. Moreover, after the model is saved to a file, it is also important to know how to load the saved model in order to use it to make predictions on new data. By saving and loading a model, we allow for the model to be reused at any moment and through many different means.

Saving a Model

The process of saving a model is also called **serialization**, and it has become increasingly important, due to the popularity of neural networks that use many variables which are randomly initialized every time the model is trained, as well as due to the introduction of bigger and more complex datasets that make the training process last for days, weeks, and sometimes months.

Considering this, the process of saving a model helps to optimize the use of machine learning solutions by standardizing the results to the saved version of the model. It also saves time, as it allows you to directly apply the saved model to new data, without the need for retraining.

There are two main ways to save a trained model, one of which will be explained in this section. The `pickle` module is the standard way to serialize objects in Python, and it works by implementing a powerful algorithm that serializes the model and then saves it as a `.pkl` file.

> **Note**
>
> The other module that's available for saving a trained model is `joblib`, which is part of the SciPy ecosystem.

However, take into account that models are only saved when they are meant to be used in future projects or for future predictions. When a machine learning project is developed to understand the current data, there is no need to save it, as the analysis will be performed after the model has been trained.

Exercise 19: Saving a Trained Model

For the following exercise, we will use the Fertility Dataset that we downloaded previously. A neural network will be trained over the training data, and then saved. Follow these steps to complete this exercise:

1. Open a Jupyter Notebook to implement this exercise and import **pandas**:

   ```
   import pandas as pd
   ```

2. Load the Fertility Dataset and split the data into a features matrix **X** and a target matrix **Y**. Use the **header = None** argument, since the dataset does not have a header row.

   ```
   data = pd.read_csv("datasets/fertility_Diagnosis.csv", header=None)

   X = data.iloc[:,:9]
   Y = data.iloc[:,9]
   ```

3. Train a Multilayer Perceptron Classifier over the data. Set the number of iterations to, 1200 to avoid getting a warning message indicating that the default number of iterations is insufficient to achieve convergence:

   ```
   from sklearn.neural_network import MLPClassifier
   model = MLPClassifier(max_iter = 1200)
   model.fit(X,Y)
   ```

4. Import the **pickle** and **os** modules, as follows:

   ```
   import pickle
   import os
   ```

   The first module (**pickle**), as explained before, will be used to save the trained model. The **os** module is used to locate the current path of the Jupyter Notebook in order to save the model in the same location.

5. Serialize the model and save it in a file named **model_exercise.pkl**. Use the following code:

   ```
   path = os.getcwd() + "/model_exercise.pkl"
   file = open(path, "wb")
   pickle.dump(model, file)
   ```

In the preceding snippet, the **path** variable contains the path of the file that will hold the serialized model, where the first element locates the path, and the second element defines the name of the file to be saved. The **file** variable is used to create a file that will be saved in the desired path and has the file mode set to **wb**, which stands for **write** and **binary** (this is the way the serialized model must be written). Finally, the **dump** method is applied over the **pickle** module. It takes the model that was created previously, serializes it, and then saves it to the created file.

Congratulations! You have successfully saved a trained model.

Loading a Model

The process of loading a model is also known as **deserialization**, and it consists of taking the previously saved file, deserializing it, and then loading it into a code or terminal, so that you can use the model on new data. The **pickle** module is also used to load the model.

It is worth mentioning that the model does not need to be loaded in the same code file where it was trained and saved; on the contrary, it is meant to be loaded in any other file. This is mainly because the **load** method of the **pickle** library will return the model in a variable that will be used to apply the **predict** method.

When loading a model, it is important to not only import the **pickle** and **os** modules like we did before, but also the class of the algorithm that is used to train the model. For instance, to load a neural network model, it is necessary to import the **MLPClassifier** class, under the **neural_network** module.

Exercise 20: Loading a Saved Model

In the following exercise, using a different Jupyter Notebook, we will load the previously trained model and perform a prediction:

1. Open a Jupyter Notebook to implement this exercise.
2. Import the **pickle** and **os** modules. Also, import the **MLPCLassifier** class:

```
import pickle
import os
from sklearn.neural_network import MLPClassifier
```

3. Use **pickle** to load the saved model, as follows:

```
path = os.getcwd() + "/model_exercise.pkl"
file = open(path, "rb")
model = pickle.load(file)
```

Here, the **path** variable is also used to store the path of the **file** model. Next, the **file** variable is used to open the file using the **rb** file mode, which stands for **read** and **binary**. Finally, the **load** method is applied over the **pickle** module to deserialize and load the model into the **model** variable.

4. Use the loaded model to make a prediction for an individual, with the following values as the values for the features: -0.33, 0.67, 1, 1, 0, 0, 0.8, -1, 0.5.

   Store the output obtained by applying the **predict** method to the **model** variable, in a variable named **pred**:

   ```
   pred = model.predict([[-0.33,0.67,1,1,0,0,0.8,-1,0.5]])
   ```

   By printing the **pred** variable, we get the value of the prediction as equal to **0**, which means that the individual has an altered diagnosis.

Congratulations! You have successfully loaded a saved model.

Activity 17: Saving and Loading the Final Model for the Bank Marketing Dataset

Consider the following scenario: your boss loves the work that you have done so far and wants you to save the model, so that it can be used in the future without the need to retrain the model and without the risk of getting different results each time. For this purpose, you need to save and load the model that you created in the previous activity.

> **Note**
>
> The following activity will be divided into two parts.
>
> The first part carries out the process of saving the model, and will be performed using the same Jupyter Notebook from the previous activity. The second part consists of loading the saved model, which will be done using a different Jupyter Notebook.

Follow these steps to complete this activity:

1. Open the Jupyter Notebook with the preprocessed Bank Marketing Dataset loaded and the models trained.
2. For learning purposes, take the model that you selected as the best model, and run it a couple of times.

> **Note**
>
> Check that you are not using a **random_state** argument, so that you can get different results each time.

   Make sure that you run the calculation of the precision metric every time you run the model, in order to see the difference in performance that's achieved in every run. Feel free to stop when you think you have landed at a model with good performance, out of all the results you get from previous runs.

3. Save the model in a file named **final_model.pkl**.

> **Note**
>
> Make sure that you use the **os** module to save the model in the same path as the current Jupyter Notebook. This way, you will be able to find a new file in the folder after saving the model.

4. Open a new Jupyter Notebook and import the required modules and class.
5. Load the model.
6. Perform a prediction for an individual, using the following values: 42, 2, 0, 0, 1, 2, 1, 0, 5, 8, 380, 1, -1, 0.

> **Note**
>
> The solution for this activity can be found on page 214.

Regardless of the model chosen, the prediction for the sample individual should be **0 (No)**.

Interacting with a Trained Model

Once the model has been created and saved, it is time for the last step of building a comprehensive machine learning program: allowing for easy interaction with the model. This step not only allows for the reusability of the model, but also introduces efficiency to the implementation of machine learning solutions, by allowing you to perform classifications using just input data.

There are several ways to interact with a model, and the decision made between one or the other depends on the nature of the user (the individuals that will be making use of the model on a regular basis). Machine learning projects can be accessed in different ways, some of which require the use of an API, an online or offline program, or a website.

Moreover, once the channel is defined based on the preference or expertise of the users, it is important to code the connection between the final user and the model, which could be either a function or a class that deserializes the model and loads it, then performs the classification, and ultimately, returns an output that is displayed again to the user.

The following diagram displays the relationship built between the channel and the model, where the first image represents the model, the second is the function or class (the intermediary) performing the connection, and the final image is the channel. Here, as was explained previously, the channel feeds the input data to the intermediary, which then feeds the information into the model to perform a classification. The output from the classification is sent back to the intermediary, which passes it along the channel in order to be displayed:

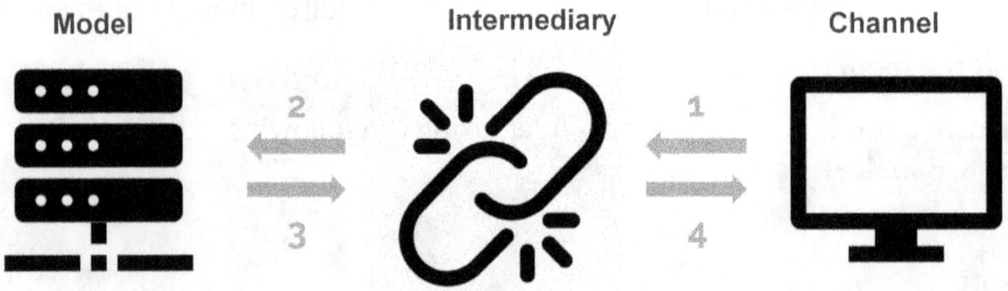

Figure 6.5: Illustration of the interaction between the user and the model

Exercise 21: Creating a Class and a Channel to Interact with a Trained Model

In the following exercise, we will create a class in a text editor that takes the input data and feeds it to the model. Additionally, we will create a form in a Jupyter Notebook, where users can input the data and obtain a prediction.

To create a class in a text editor, follow these steps:

1. Open the text editor of your preference.
2. Import **pandas**, **pickle**, and **os**, along with the Multilayer Perceptron Classifier class:

```
import pandas as pd
import pickle
import os
from sklearn.neural_network import MLPClassifier
```

3. Create a class object and name it **NN_Model**:

```
Class NN_Model(object):
```

4. Inside of the class, create an initializer method that loads the file containing the saved model (**model_exercise.pkl**) into the code:

```
def __init__(self):
  path = os.getcwd() + "/model_exercise.pkl"
  file = open(path, "rb")
  self.model = pickle.load(file)
```

> **Note**
>
> Remember to indent the method inside of the class object.

As a general rule, all the methods inside a class object must have the argument **self**. On the other hand, when defining the variable of the model using the **self** statement, it is possible to make use of the variable in any other method of the same class.

5. Create a **predict** method that takes in all of the features as arguments. It should take in the feature values and input them as arguments to the **predict** method, so that it can feed them into the model:

```
def predict(self, season, age, childish, trauma, surgical, fevers,
alcohol, smoking, sitting):
  X = [[season, age, childish, trauma, surgical, fevers, alcohol, smoking,
sitting]]
  return self.model.predict(X)
```

6. Save the code as a Python file (**.py**) and name it **exerciseClass.py**. The name of this file will be used to load the class into the Jupyter Notebook for the following steps.

Now, let's code the frontend solution of the program, which includes creating a form where users can input data and obtain a prediction:

1. Open a Jupyter Notebook to code the frontend solution of the machine learning program.

2. To import the model class that we created previously, use the following code snippet:

```
from exerciseClass import NN_Model
```

3. Initialize the model and store it in a variable named **model**:

```
model = NN_Model()
```

4. Create a set of variables where the user can input the value for each feature, which will then be fed to the model. Use the following values:

```
a = 1       # season in which the analysis was performed
b = 0.56    # age at the time of the analysis
c = 1       # childish disease
d = 1       # accident or serious trauma
e = 1       # surgical intervention
f = 0       # high fevers in the last year
g = 1       # frequency of alcohol consumption
h = -1      # smoking habit
i = 0.63    # number of hours spent sitting per day
```

5. Perform a prediction by using the **predict** method on the model variable. Input the feature values as arguments, taking into account that you must name them in the same way that you did when creating the **predict** function in the text editor:

```
pred = model.predict(season=a, age=b, childish=c, trauma=d, surgical=e,
fevers=f, alcohol=g, smoking=h, sitting=i)
```

Congratulations! You have successfully created a function and a channel to interact with your model.

Activity 18: Allowing Interaction with the Bank Marketing Dataset Model

Consider the following scenario: after seeing the results that you presented, your boss has asked you to build a very simple way for him to test the model with data that he will receive over the book of the next month. If all the tests work well, he will be asking you to launch the program in a more effective way. Hence, you have decided to share a Jupyter Notebook with your boss, where he can just input the information and get a prediction.

> **Note**
>
> The following activity will be developed in two parts. The first part will involve building the class that connects the channel and the model, and will be developed using a text editor. The second part will be the creation of the channel, and will be done in a Jupyter Notebook.

Follow these steps to complete this activity:

1. In a text editor, create a class object that contains two main methods. One should be an initializer that loads the model, and the other should be a **`predict`** method, wherein the data is fed to the model to retrieve an output.
2. In a Jupyter Notebook, import and initialize the class that you created in the last step. Next, create the variables that will hold the values for the features, and use the following values: 42, 2, 0, 0, 1, 2, 1, 0, 5, 8, 380, 1, -1, 0.
3. Perform a prediction by applying the **`predict`** method.

> **Note**
>
> The solution for this activity can be found on page 215.

The prediction for the sample individual should be equal to **`0`**, which is the numeric form of **`No`**.

Summary

This chapter wraps up all of the concepts and techniques that are required to successfully train a machine learning model based on training data. In this chapter, we introduced the idea of building a comprehensive machine learning program that not only accounts for the stages involved in the preparation of the dataset and creation of the ideal model, but also the stage related to making the model accessible for future use, which is accomplished by carrying out three main processes: saving the model, loading the model, and creating a channel that allows users to easily interact with the model and obtain an outcome. The **pickle** module was also introduced in this regard.

Further, to make the model accessible to users, the ideal channel (for example, an API, an application, a website or a form) needs to be selected according to the type of user that will interact with the model. Then, an intermediary needs to be programmed, which can connect the channel with the model. This intermediary is usually in the form of a function or a class.

The main objective of this book was to introduce scikit-learn's library as a way to work with machine learning in a simpler manner. After discussing the importance of and the different techniques involved in data exploration and preprocessing, this book divided this knowledge into the two main areas of machine learning: supervised learning and unsupervised learning. We discussed the various algorithms used in each. Finally, in this book, we explained the importance of measuring the performance of models by performing error analysis, in order improve the overall performance of the model on unseen data, and ultimately, choosing the model that best represents the data. This final model should be saved, so that you can use it in the future for visualizations, or to perform predictions.

Appendix

About

This section is included to assist the students to perform the activities present in the book. It includes detailed steps that are to be performed by the students to complete and achieve the objectives of the book.

Chapter 1: Introduction to scikit-learn

Activity 1: Selecting a Target Feature and Creating a Target Matrix

1. Load the **titanic** dataset using the seaborn library. First, import the seaborn library, and then use the **load_dataset("titanic")** function:

   ```
   import seaborn as sns
   titanic = sns.load_dataset('titanic')
   titanic.head(10)
   ```

   Next, print out the top 10 instances; this should match the below screenshot:

	survived	pclass	sex	age	sibsp	parch	fare	embarked	class	who	adult_male	deck	embark_town	alive	alone
0	0	3	male	22.0	1	0	7.2500	S	Third	man	True	NaN	Southampton	no	False
1	1	1	female	38.0	1	0	71.2833	C	First	woman	False	C	Cherbourg	yes	False
2	1	3	female	26.0	0	0	7.9250	S	Third	woman	False	NaN	Southampton	yes	True
3	1	1	female	35.0	1	0	53.1000	S	First	woman	False	C	Southampton	yes	False
4	0	3	male	35.0	0	0	8.0500	S	Third	man	True	NaN	Southampton	no	True
5	0	3	male	NaN	0	0	8.4583	Q	Third	man	True	NaN	Queenstown	no	True
6	0	1	male	54.0	0	0	51.8625	S	First	man	True	E	Southampton	no	True
7	0	3	male	2.0	3	1	21.0750	S	Third	child	False	NaN	Southampton	no	False
8	1	3	female	27.0	0	2	11.1333	S	Third	woman	False	NaN	Southampton	yes	False
9	1	2	female	14.0	1	0	30.0708	C	Second	child	False	NaN	Cherbourg	yes	False

Figure 1.23: An image showing the first 10 instances of the Titanic dataset

2. The preferred target feature could be either **survived** or **alive**. This is mainly because both of them label whether a person survived the crash. For the following steps, the variable chosen is **survived**. However, choosing **alive** will not affect the final shape of the variables.

3. Create a variable, **X**, to store the features, by using **drop()**. As explained previously, the selected target feature is **survived**, which is why it is dropped from the features matrix.

   Create a variable, **Y**, to store the target matrix. Use indexing to access only the value from the column **survived**:

   ```
   X = titanic.drop('survived',axis = 1)
   Y = titanic['survived']
   ```

4. Print out the shape of variable **X**, as follows:

```
X.shape
(891, 14)
```

Do the same for variable **Y**:

```
Y.shape
(891,)
```

Activity 2: Preprocessing an Entire Dataset

1. Load the dataset and create the features and target matrices:

```
import seaborn as sns
titanic = sns.load_dataset('titanic')
X = titanic[['sex','age','fare','class','embark_town','alone']]
Y = titanic['survived']
X.shape
(891, 6)
```

2. Check for missing values in all features.

As we did previously, use **isnull()** to determine whether a value is missing, and use **sum()** to sum up the occurrences of missing values along each feature:

```
print("Sex: " + str(X['sex'].isnull().sum()))
print("Age: " + str(X['age'].isnull().sum()))
print("Fare: " + str(X['fare'].isnull().sum()))
print("Class: " + str(X['class'].isnull().sum()))
print("Embark town: " + str(X['embark_town'].isnull().sum()))
print("Alone: " + str(X['alone'].isnull().sum()))
```

The output will look as follows:

```
Sex: 0
Age: 177
Fare: 0
Class: 0
Embark town: 2
Alone: 0
```

As you can see from the preceding screenshot, only two features contain missing values: **age** and **embark_town**.

3. As **age** has many missing values that accounts for almost 20% of the total, the values should be replaced. Mean imputation methodology will be applied, as shown in the following code:

```
#Age: missing values
mean = X['age'].mean()
mean = mean.round()
X['age'].fillna(mean,inplace = True)
```

```
/home/hyatt/Desktop/VirtualEnvs/explore_data/lib/python3.5/site-packages/pandas/core/generic.py:5430: Sett
ingWithCopyWarning:
A value is trying to be set on a copy of a slice from a DataFrame

See the caveats in the documentation: http://pandas.pydata.org/pandas-docs/stable/indexing.html#indexing-v
iew-versus-copy
  self._update_inplace(new_data)
```

Figure 1.24: A screenshot displaying the output of the preceding code

After calculating the mean, the missing values are replaced by it using the **fillna()** function.

> **Note**
>
> The preceding warning may appear as the values are being replaced over a slice of the DataFrame. This happens because the variable **X** is created as a slice of the entire DataFrame **titanic**. As **X** is the variable that matters for the current exercise, it is not an issue to only replace the values over the slice and not over the entire DataFrame.

4. Given that the number of missing values in the **embark_town** feature is low, the instances are eliminated from the features matrix:

> **Note**
>
> To eliminate the missing values from the **embark_town** feature, it is required to eliminate the entire instance (observation) from the matrix.

```
# Embark_town: missing values
X = X[X['embark_town'].notnull()]
X.shape
(889, 6)
```

The **notnull()** function detects all non-missing values over the object in question. In this case, the function is used to obtain all non-missing values from the **embark_town** feature. Then, indexing is used to retrieve those values from the entire matrix (**X**).

5. Discover the outliers present in the numeric features. Let's use three standard deviations as the measure to calculate the min and max threshold for numeric features. Using the formula that we have learned, the min and max threshold are calculated and compared against the min and max values of the feature:

```
feature = "age"
print("Min threshold: " + str(X[feature].mean() - (3 * X[feature].
std())),"  Min val: " + str(X[feature].min()))
print("Max threshold: " + str(X[feature].mean() + (3 * X[feature].
std())),"  Max val: " + str(X[feature].max()))
```

The values obtained for the above code are shown here:

```
Min threshold: -9.194052030619016   Min val: 0.42
Max threshold: 68.62075619259876   Max val: 80.0
```

Use the following code to calculate the min and max threshold for the **fare** feature:

```
feature = "fare"
print("Min threshold: " + str(X[feature].mean() - (3 * X[feature].
std())),"  Min val: " + str(X[feature].min()))
print("Max threshold: " + str(X[feature].mean() + (3 * X[feature].
std())),"  Max val: " + str(X[feature].max()))
```

The values obtained for the above code are shown here:

```
Min threshold: -116.99583207273355   Min val: 0.0
Max threshold: 181.1891938275142   Max val: 512.3292
```

As you can see from the preceding screenshots, both features stay inside the range at the lower end but go outside the range with the max values.

6. The total count of outliers for the features **age** and **fare** are 7 and 20, respectively. Neither amount represents a high percentage of the total number of values, which is why outliers are eliminated from the features matrix. The following snippet can be used to eliminate the outliers and print the shape of the resulting matrix:

```
# Age: outliers
max_age = X["age"].mean() + (3 * X["age"].std())
X = X[X["age"] <= max_age]
X.shape
(882, 6)

# Fare: outliers
max_fare = X["fare"].mean() + (3 * X["fare"].std())
X = X[X["fare"] <= max_fare]
X.shape
(862, 6)
```

7. Discover outliers present in text features. The **value_counts()** function is used to count the occurrence of the classes in each feature:

```
feature = "alone"
X[feature].value_counts()
True     522
False    340

feature = "class"
X[feature].value_counts()
Third     489
First     190
Second    183

feature = "alone"
X[feature].value_counts()
True     522
False    340

feature = "embark_town"
X[feature].value_counts()
Southampton    632
Cherbourg      154
Queenstown      76
```

None of the classes for any of the features are considered to be outliers, as they all represent over 5% of the entire dataset.

8. Convert all text features into their numeric representations. Use scikit-learn's **LabelEncoder** class, as shown in the following code:

```
from sklearn.preprocessing import LabelEncoder
enc = LabelEncoder()
X["sex"] = enc.fit_transform(X['sex'].astype('str'))
X["class"] = enc.fit_transform(X['class'].astype('str'))
X["embark_town"] = enc.fit_transform(X['embark_town'].astype('str'))
X["alone"] = enc.fit_transform(X['alone'].astype('str'))
```

9. Print out the top 5 instances of the features matrix to view the result of the conversion:

```
X.head()
```

	sex	age	fare	class	embark_town	alone
0	1	22.0	7.2500	2	2	0
1	0	38.0	71.2833	0	0	0
2	0	26.0	7.9250	2	2	1
3	0	35.0	53.1000	0	2	0
4	1	35.0	8.0500	2	2	1

Figure 1.25: A screenshot displaying the first five instances of the features matrix

10. Finally, apply normalization (or standardization) to the matrix.

As you can see from the following code, the formula for normalization is only applied to those features that need normalizing. Given that normalization rescales the values between 0 and 1, all the features that have already met that condition do not need to be normalized:

```
X["age"] = (X["age"] - X["age"].min())/(X["age"].max()-X["age"].min())
X["fare"] = (X["fare"] - X["fare"].min())/(X["fare"].max()-X["fare"].
min())
X["class"] = (X["class"] - X["class"].min())/(X["class"].max()-X["class"].
min())
X["embark_town"] = (X["embark_town"] - X["embark_town"].min())/(X["embark_
town"].max()-X["embark_town"].min())
X.head(10)
```

The top 10 rows of the final output are shown in the following screenshot:

	sex	age	fare	class	embark_town	alone
0	1	0.329064	0.043975	1.0	1.0	0
1	0	0.573041	0.432369	0.0	0.0	0
2	0	0.390058	0.048069	1.0	1.0	1
3	0	0.527295	0.322078	0.0	1.0	0
4	1	0.527295	0.048827	1.0	1.0	1
5	1	0.451052	0.051304	1.0	0.5	1
6	1	0.817017	0.314572	0.0	1.0	1
7	1	0.024093	0.127831	1.0	1.0	0
8	0	0.405306	0.067529	1.0	1.0	0
9	0	0.207075	0.182395	0.5	0.0	0

Figure 1.26: A screenshot displaying the first 10 instances of the normalized dataset

Chapter 2: Unsupervised Learning: Real-life Applications

Activity 3: Using Data Visualization to Aid the Preprocessing Process

1. Load the previously downloaded dataset by using the Pandas function **read_csv()**. Store the dataset in a Pandas DataFrame named **data**:

```
import pandas as pd
import matplotlib.pyplot as plt
import numpy as np
np.random.seed(0)
```

First, import the required libraries. Then, feed the dataset path to the Pandas function's **read_csv()**:

```
data = pd.read_csv("datasets/wholesale_customers_data.csv")
```

2. Check for missing values in your DataFrame. Using the **isnull()** function plus the **sum()** function, count the missing values of the entire dataset at once:

```
data.isnull().sum()
```

```
Channel             0
Region              0
Fresh               0
Milk                0
Grocery             0
Frozen              0
Detergents_Paper    0
Delicassen          0
dtype: int64
```

Figure 2.16: A screenshot showing the number of missing values in the DataFrame

As you can see from the preceding screenshot, there are no missing values in the dataset.

3. Check for outliers in your DataFrame. Using the technique you learned in the previous chapter, label those values that fall outside of three standard deviations from the mean as outliers. The following code snippet allows you to look for outliers in the entire set of features at once. However, another valid method would be to check for outliers one feature at a time:

```
outliers = {}
for i in range(data.shape[1]):
  min_t = data[data.columns[i]].mean() - (3 * data[data.columns[i]].std())
  max_t = data[data.columns[i]].mean() + (3 * data[data.columns[i]].std())
  count = 0
  for j in data[data.columns[i]]:
    if j < min_t or j > max_t:
      count += 1
  outliers[data.columns[i]] = [count,data.shape[0]-count]
print(outliers)
```

The count of outliers for each of the features is shown in the following figure:

```
{'Detergents_Paper': [10, 430], 'Grocery': [7, 433], 'Frozen': [6, 434], 'Milk': [9, 431], 'Fresh': [7, 43
3], 'Region': [0, 440], 'Channel': [0, 440], 'Delicassen': [4, 436]}
```

Figure 2.17: A screenshot showing the output of the preceding code snippet

As you can see from the preceding screenshot, some features do have outliers. Considering that there are only a few outliers for each feature, there are two possible ways to handle them.

First, you could decide to delete the outliers. This decision can be supported by displaying a histogram for the features with outliers:

```
plt.hist(data["Fresh"])
plt.show()
```

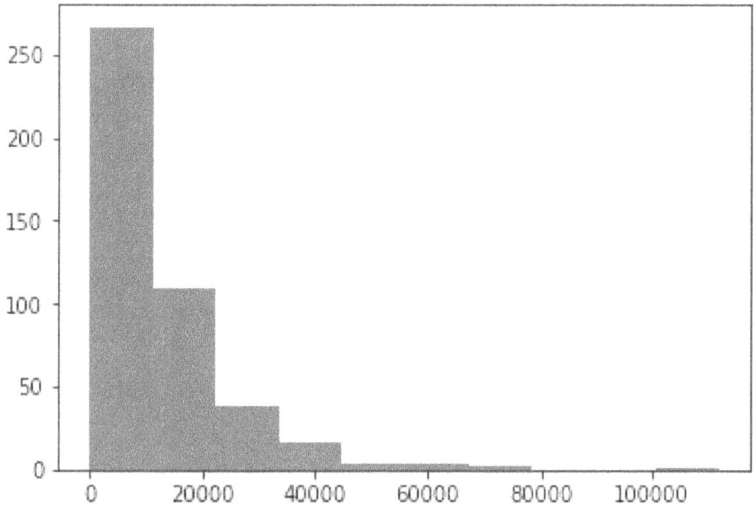

Figure 2.18: An example histogram plot for the "Fresh" feature

For instance, for the feature named **Fresh**, it can be seen through the histogram that most instances are represented by values below 40,000. Hence, deleting the instances above that value will not affect the performance of the model.

On the other hand, the second approach would be to leave the outliers as they are, considering that they do not represent a large portion of the dataset, which can be supported with data visualization tools using a pie chart. See the code and the output that follow:

```
plt.figure(figsize=(8,8))
plt.pie(outliers["Detergents_Paper"],autopct="%.2f")
plt.show()
```

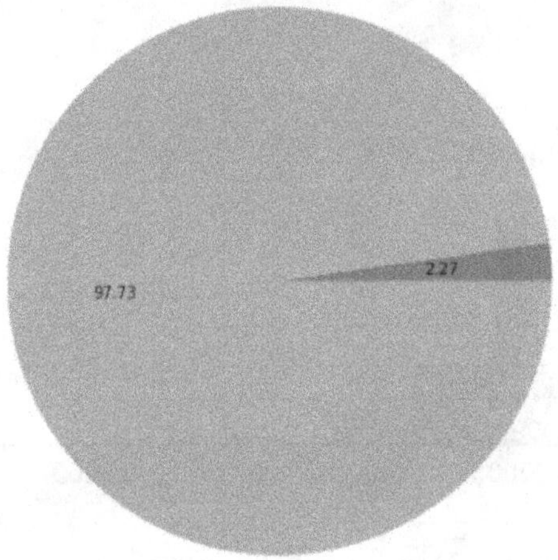

Figure 2.19: A pie chart showing the participation of outliers from the **Detergents_papers** feature in the dataset

The preceding diagram shows the participation of the outliers from the **Detergents_papers** feature, which was the feature with the most outliers in the dataset. Only 2.27% of the values are outliers, a value so low that it will not affect the performance of the model either.

4. Rescale the data. For this solution, the formula for standardization has been used. Note that the formula can be applied to the entire dataset at once, instead of being applied individually to each feature:

```
data_standardized = (data - data.mean())/data.std()
data_standardized.head()
```

	Channel	Region	Fresh	Milk	Grocery	Frozen	Detergents_Paper	Delicassen
0	1.447005	0.589997	0.052873	0.522972	-0.041068	-0.588697	-0.043519	-0.066264
1	1.447005	0.589997	-0.390857	0.543839	0.170125	-0.269829	0.086309	0.089050
2	1.447005	0.589997	-0.446521	0.408073	-0.028125	-0.137379	0.133080	2.240742
3	-0.689512	0.589997	0.099998	-0.623310	-0.392530	0.686363	-0.498021	0.093305
4	1.447005	0.589997	0.839284	-0.052337	-0.079266	0.173661	-0.231654	1.297870

Figure 2.20: A table showing the first five instances of the standardized dataset

Activity 4: Applying the k-means Algorithm to a Dataset

1. Open the Jupyter Notebook that you used for the previous activity. There, you should have imported all the required libraries and stored the dataset in a variable named **data**. The standardized data should look as follows:

```
data_standardized = (data - data.mean())/data.std()
data_standardized.head()
```

	Channel	Region	Fresh	Milk	Grocery	Frozen	Detergents_Paper	Delicassen
0	1.447005	0.589997	0.052873	0.522972	-0.041068	-0.588697	-0.043519	-0.066264
1	1.447005	0.589997	-0.390857	0.543839	0.170125	-0.269829	0.086309	0.089050
2	1.447005	0.589997	-0.446521	0.408073	-0.028125	-0.137379	0.133080	2.240742
3	-0.689512	0.589997	0.099998	-0.623310	-0.392530	0.686363	-0.498021	0.093305
4	1.447005	0.589997	0.839284	-0.052337	-0.079266	0.173661	-0.231654	1.297870

Figure 2.21: A screenshot displaying the first five instances of the standardized dataset

2. Calculate the average distance of data points from its centroid in relation to the number of clusters. Based on this distance, select the appropriate number of clusters to train the model to.

   First, import the algorithm class:

```
from sklearn.cluster import KMeans
```

Next, using the code in the following snippet, calculate the average distance of data points from its centroid based on the number of clusters created:

```
ideal_k = []
for i in range(1,21):
  est_kmeans = KMeans(n_clusters=i)
  est_kmeans.fit(data_standardized)

  ideal_k.append([i,est_kmeans.inertia_])
ideal_k = np.array(ideal_k)
```

Finally, plot the relation to find the breaking point of the line, and select the number of clusters:

```
plt.plot(ideal_k[:,0],ideal_k[:,1])
plt.show()
```

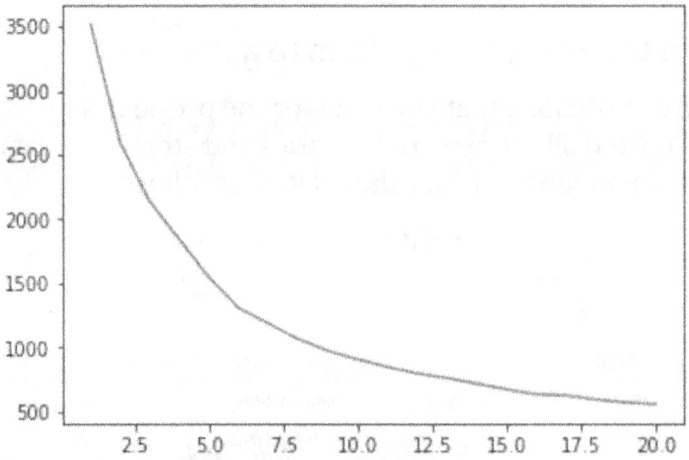

Figure 2.22: The output of the plot function used

3. Train the model and assign a cluster to each data point in your dataset. Plot the results.

   To train the model, use the following code:

```
est_kmeans = KMeans(n_clusters=6)
est_kmeans.fit(data_standardized)
pred_kmeans = est_kmeans.predict(data_standardized)
```

   The number of clusters selected is 6; however, since there is no exact breaking point, values between 5 and 10 are also acceptable.

Finally, plot the results of the clustering process. As the dataset contains eight different features, choose two features to draw at once, as shown in the following code:

```
plt.subplots(1, 2, sharex='col', sharey='row', figsize=(16,8))
plt.scatter(data.iloc[:,5], data.iloc[:,3], c=pred_kmeans, s=20)
plt.xlim([0, 20000])
plt.ylim([0,20000])
plt.xlabel('Frozen')
plt.subplot(1, 2, 1)
plt.scatter(data.iloc[:,4], data.iloc[:,3], c=pred_kmeans, s=20)
plt.xlim([0, 20000])
plt.ylim([0,20000])
plt.xlabel('Grocery')
plt.ylabel('Milk')
plt.show()
```

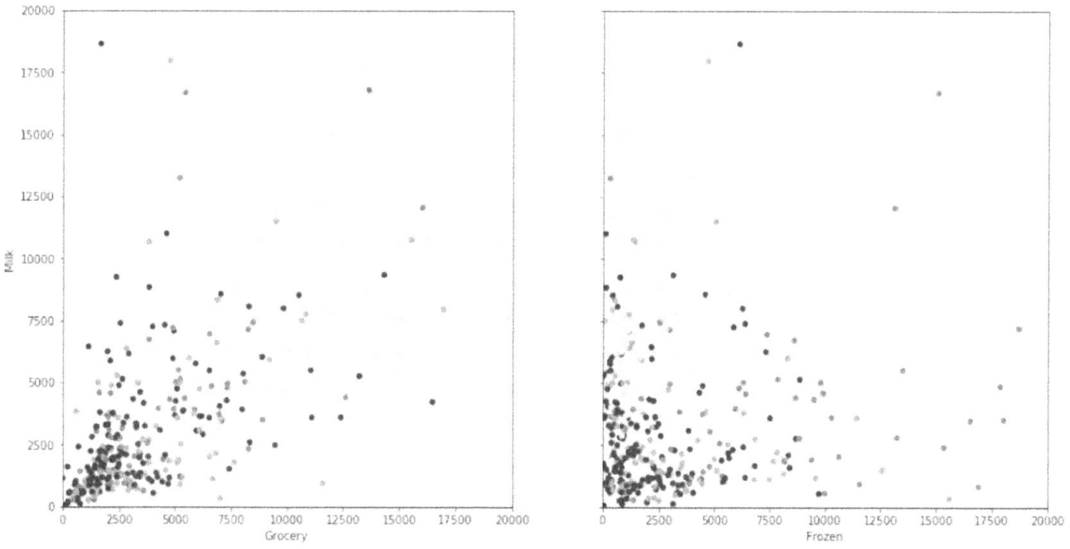

Figure 2.23: Two example plots obtained after the clustering process

The **`subplots()`** function from Matplotlib has been used to plot two scatter graphs at a time.

As can be seen from the plots, there is no obvious visual relation due to the fact that we are only able to use two of the eight features present in the dataset. However, the final output of the model creates six different clusters that represent six different profiles of clients.

Activity 5: Applying the Mean-Shift Algorithm to a Dataset

1. Open the Jupyter Notebook that you used for the previous activity.
2. Train the model and assign a cluster to each data point in your dataset. Plot the results.

   First, do not forget to import the algorithm class:

   ```
   from sklearn.cluster import MeanShift
   ```

   To train the model, use the following code:

   ```
   est_meanshift = MeanShift(0.4)
   est_meanshift.fit(data_standardized)
   pred_meanshift = est_meanshift.predict(data_standardized)
   ```

   The model was trained using a bandwidth of 0.4. However, feel free to test other values to see how the result changes.

   Finally, plot the results of the clustering process. As the dataset contains eight different features, choose two features to draw at once, as shown in the snippet below. Similar to the previous activity, the separation between clusters is not visually seen due to the capability to only draw two out of the eight features:

   ```
   plt.subplots(1, 2, sharex='col', sharey='row', figsize=(16,8))
   plt.scatter(data.iloc[:,5], data.iloc[:,3], c=pred_meanshift, s=20)
   plt.xlim([0, 20000])
   plt.ylim([0,20000])
   plt.xlabel('Frozen')
   plt.subplot(1, 2, 1)
   plt.scatter(data.iloc[:,4], data.iloc[:,3], c=pred_meanshift, s=20)
   plt.xlim([0, 20000])
   plt.ylim([0,20000])
   plt.xlabel('Grocery')
   plt.ylabel('Milk')
   plt.show()
   ```

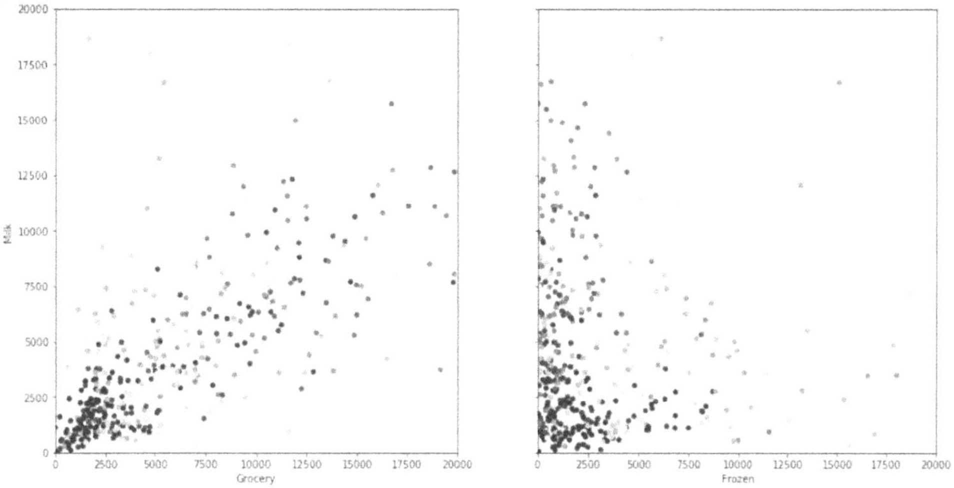

Figure 2.24: Example plots obtained at the end of the process

Activity 6: Applying the DBSCAN Algorithm to the Dataset

1. Open the Jupyter Notebook that you used for the previous activity.
2. Train the model and assign a cluster to each data point in your dataset. Plot the results.

   First, do not forget to import the algorithm class:

   ```
   from sklearn.cluster import DBSCAN
   ```

   To train the model, use the following code:

   ```
   est_dbscan = DBSCAN(eps=0.8)
   pred_dbscan = est_dbscan.fit_predict(data_standardized)
   ```

   The model was trained using an **epsilon** value of **0.8**. However, feel free to test other values to see how the results change.

Finally, plot the results of the clustering process. As the dataset contains eight different features, choose two features to draw at once, as shown in the following code:

```
plt.subplots(1, 2, sharex='col', sharey='row', figsize=(16,8))
plt.scatter(data.iloc[:,5], data.iloc[:,3], c=pred_dbscan, s=20)
plt.xlim([0, 20000])
plt.ylim([0,20000])
plt.xlabel('Frozen')
plt.subplot(1, 2, 1)
plt.scatter(data.iloc[:,4], data.iloc[:,3], c=pred_dbscan, s=20)
plt.xlim([0, 20000])
plt.ylim([0,20000])
plt.xlabel('Grocery')
plt.ylabel('Milk')
plt.show()
```

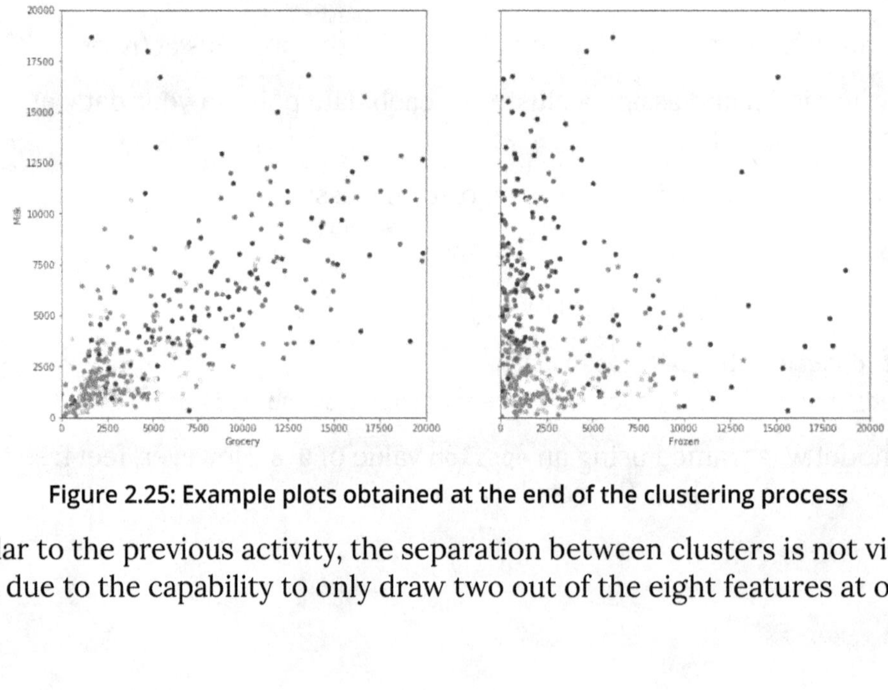

Figure 2.25: Example plots obtained at the end of the clustering process

Similar to the previous activity, the separation between clusters is not visually seen due to the capability to only draw two out of the eight features at once.

Activity 7: Measuring and Comparing the Performance of the Algorithms

1. Open the Jupyter Notebook that you used for the previous activity.
2. Calculate both the Silhouette Coefficient score and the Calinski–Harabasz index for all the models that you trained previously.

   First, do not forget to import the metrics:

   ```
   from sklearn.metrics import silhouette_score
   from sklearn.metrics import silhouette_score
   ```

   Calculate the Silhouette Coefficient score for all the algorithms, as shown in the following code:

   ```
   kmeans_score = silhouette_score(data_standardized, pred_kmeans,
   metric='euclidean')
   meanshift_score = silhouette_score(data_standardized, pred_meanshift,
   metric='euclidean')
   dbscan_score = silhouette_score(data_standardized, pred_dbscan,
   metric='euclidean')
   print(kmeans_score, meanshift_score, dbscan_score)
   ```

   The scores come to be around 0.355, 0.093, and 0.168 for the k-means, Mean-Shift, and DBSCAN algorithms, respectively.

   Finally, calculate the Calinski–Harabasz index for all the algorithms. The following is a snippet of the code:

   ```
   kmeans_score = calinski_harabaz_score(data_standardized, pred_kmeans)
   meanshift_score = calinski_harabaz_score(data_standardized, pred_
   meanshift)
   dbscan_score = calinski_harabaz_score(data_standardized, pred_dbscan)
   print(kmeans_score, meanshift_score, dbscan_score)
   ```

   The scores come to be approximately 139.8, 112.9, and 42.45 for the three algorithms in the respective order in the code snippet.

   By quickly looking at the results obtained for both metrics, it is possible to conclude that the k-means algorithm outperforms the other models, and hence, should be the one selected to solve the data problem.

Chapter 3: Supervised Learning: Key Steps

Activity 8: Data Partition over a Handwritten Digit Dataset

1. Import the **digits** toy dataset using scikit-learn's **datasets** package and create a Pandas DataFrame containing the features and target matrices. Use the following code:

   ```
   from sklearn.datasets import load_digits
   digits = load_digits()

   import pandas as pd
   X = pd.DataFrame(digits.data)
   Y = pd.DataFrame(digits.target)
   ```

   The shape of your features and target matrix should be as follows, respectively:

   ```
   (1797,64) (1797,1)
   ```

2. Choose the appropriate approach for splitting the dataset and split it.

   Conventional split approach (60/20/20%)

   Using the **train_test_split** function, split the data into an initial train set and a test set:

   ```
   from sklearn.model_selection import train_test_split

   X_new, X_test, Y_new, Y_test = train_test_split(X, Y, test_size=0.2)
   ```

   The shape of the sets that you created should be as follows:

   ```
   (1437,64) (360,64) (1437,1) (360,1)
   ```

   Next, calculate the value of the **test_size**, which sets the size of the dev set equal to the size of the test set that was created previously:

   ```
   dev_size = 360/1437
   ```

   The result of the preceding operation is 0.2505.

   Finally, split **X_new** and **Y_new** into the final train and dev sets. Use the following code:

   ```
   X_train, X_dev, Y_train, Y_dev = train_test_split(X_new, Y_new, test_size
   = 0.25)
   ```

The final shape of all sets is shown here:

```
X_train = (1077,64)
X_dev = (360,64)
X_test = (360,64)
Y_train = (1077,1)
Y_dev = (360,1)
Y_test = (360,1)
```

Cross-Validation Approach

Using the **train_test_split** function, split the data into an initial train set and a test set, just like you did previously:

```
from sklearn.model_selection import train_test_split

X_new_2, X_test_2, Y_new_2, Y_test_2 = train_test_split(X, Y, test_
size=0.1)
```

Using the **KFold** class, perform a 10-fold split:

```
from sklearn.model_selection import KFold

kf = Kfold(n_splits = 10)
splits = kf.split(X_new_2)
```

Remember that cross-validation performs different configuration of splits, shuffling data each time. Considering this, perform a **for** loop that will go through all the split configurations:

```
for train_index, dev_index in splits:
  X_train_2, X_dev_2 = X_new_2.iloc[train_index], X_new_2.iloc[dev_index]

  Y_train_2, Y_dev_2 = Y_new_2.iloc[train_index], Y_new_2.iloc[dev_index]
```

The code in charge of training and evaluating the model should be inside the body of the **for** loop in order to train and evaluate the model with each configuration of splits.

The final shape of the sets will be as follows:

```
X_train_2 = (1456,64)
X_dev_2 = (161,64)
X_test_2 = (180,64)
Y_train_2 = (1456,1)
Y_dev_2 = (161,1)
Y_test_2 = (180,1)
```

Activity 9: Evaluating the Performance of the Model Trained over a Handwritten Dataset

1. Import the toy dataset **boston** using scikit-learn's **datasets** package and create a Pandas DataFrame containing the features and target matrices:

```
from sklearn.datasets import load_digits
data = load_digits()

import pandas as pd
X = pd.DataFrame(data.data)
Y = pd.DataFrame(data.target)
```

2. Split the data into training and testing sets. Use 20% as the size of the testing set:

```
from sklearn.model_selection import train_test_split
X_train, X_test, Y_train, Y_test = train_test_split(X,Y, test_size = 0.1,
random_state = 0)
```

3. Train a decision tree over the train set. Then, use the model to predict the class label over the test set (hint: to train the Decision Tree, revisit *Exercise 12*):

```
from sklearn import tree
model = tree.DecisionTreeClassifier(random_state = 0)
model = model.fit(X_train, Y_train)

Y_pred = model.predict(X_test)
```

4. Use scikit-learn to construct a confusion matrix:

```
from sklearn.metrics import confusion_matrix
confusion_matrix = confusion_matrix (Y_test, Y_pred)
```

The output of the confusion matrix is shown as follows:

```
array([[24,  0,  0,  0,  0,  0,  1,  0,  0,  2],
       [ 0, 31,  0,  2,  1,  0,  1,  0,  0,  0],
       [ 1,  0, 29,  0,  0,  0,  2,  2,  1,  1],
       [ 0,  0,  2, 27,  0,  0,  0,  0,  0,  0],
       [ 1,  1,  0,  0, 26,  0,  1,  1,  0,  0],
       [ 0,  1,  1,  0,  0, 34,  0,  0,  1,  3],
       [ 1,  1,  1,  1,  1,  0, 39,  0,  0,  0],
       [ 0,  0,  0,  0,  0,  1,  1, 37,  0,  0],
       [ 1,  3,  3,  5,  0,  1,  0,  1, 24,  1],
       [ 0,  0,  1,  4,  0,  1,  0,  0,  1, 34]])
```

Figure 3.13: Output of the confusion matrix from Activity 9

5. Calculate the accuracy of the model:

```
from sklearn.metrics import accuracy_score
accuracy_score = accuracy_score(Y_test, Y_pred)
```

The accuracy is equal to 84.72%.

6. Calculate the precision and recall. Considering that both the precision and recall can only be calculated over binary data, assume that we are only interested in classifying instances as **number 6** or **any other number**:

```
Y_test_2 = Y_test[:]
Y_test_2[Y_test_2 != 6] = 1
Y_test_2[Y_test_2 == 6] = 0

Y_pred_2 = Y_pred
Y_pred_2[Y_pred_2 != 6] = 1
Y_pred_2[Y_pred_2 == 6] = 0

From sklearn.metrics import precision_score, recall_score
precision = precision_score(Y_test_2, Y_pred_2)
recall = recall_score(Y_test_2, Y_pred_2)
```

The precision and recall scores should be equal to 98.41% and 98.10%, respectively.

Activity 10: Performing Error Analysis over a Model Trained to Recognize Handwritten Digits

1. Import the **digits** toy dataset using scikit-learn's **datasets** package and create a Pandas DataFrame containing the features and target matrices:

```
from sklearn.datasets import load_digits
data = load_digits()

import pandas as pd
X = pd.DataFrame(data.data)
Y = pd.DataFrame(data.target)
```

2. Split the data into training, validation, and testing sets. Use 0.1 as the size of the test set, and an equivalent number to build a validation set of the same shape:

```
from sklearn.model_selection import train_test_split

X_new, X_test, Y_new, Y_test = train_test_split(X, Y, test_size = 0.1, random_state = 101)

X_train, X_dev, Y_train, Y_dev = train_test_split(X_new, Y_new, test_size = 0.11, random_state = 101)
```

3. Create a train/dev set for both the features and the target values that contains 89 instances/labels of the train set and 89 instances/labels of the dev set:

```
import numpy as np
np.random.seed(101)

indices_train = np.random.randint(0, len(X_train), 89)
indices_dev = np.random.randint(0, len(X_dev), 89)

X_train_dev = pd.concat([X_train.iloc[indices_train,:], X_dev.iloc[indices_dev,:]])

Y_train_dev = pd.concat([Y_train.iloc[indices_train,:], Y_dev.iloc[indices_dev,:]])
```

4. Train a decision tree over that training set data:

```
from sklearn import tree

model = tree.DecisionTreeClassifier(random_state = 101)
model = model.fit(X_train, Y_train)
```

5. Calculate the error rate for all sets of data, and determine which condition is affecting the performance of the model:

```
from sklearn.metrics import accuracy_score
X_sets = [X_train, X_train_dev, X_dev, X_test]
Y_sets = [Y_train, Y_train_dev, Y_dev, Y_test]

scores = []
for i in range(0, len(X_sets)):
  pred = model.predict(X_sets[i])
  score = accuracy_score(Y_sets[i], pred)
  scores.append(score)
```

The error rates are shown in the following table:

Set	Error
Bayes Error/Human Error	0
Training set Error	0
Train/Dev set Error	0.0562
Dev set Error	0.1180
Testing set Error	0.1167

Figure 3.14: Error rates of the Handwritten Digits model

From the preceding results of the errors, it can be concluded that the model is equally suffering from variance and data mismatch.

Chapter 4: Supervised Learning Algorithms: Predict Annual Income

Activity 11: Training a Naïve Bayes Model for our Census Income Dataset

Before working on step 1, make sure that the data has been preprocessed, as follows:

```
import pandas as pd

data = pd.read_csv("datasets/census_income_dataset.csv")

data = data.drop(["fnlwgt","education","relationship","sex", "race"],
axis=1)
```

After reading the dataset, the three variables considered irrelevant for the study are removed.

Next, the remaining qualitative variables are converted into their numerical form via the following code:

```
from sklearn.preprocessing import LabelEncoder

enc = LabelEncoder()


features_to_convert = ["workclass","marital-status","occupation","native-
country","target"]


for i in features_to_convert:

  data[i] = enc.fit_transform(data[i].astype('str'))
```

Once this is complete, you can begin with the steps of the activity:

1. Using the preprocessed Census Income Dataset, separate the features from the target by creating the variables **X** and **Y**:

   ```
   X = data.drop("target", axis=1)
   Y = data["target"]
   ```

   Note that there are several ways to achieve the separation of **X** and **Y**. Use the one that you feel most comfortable with. However, take into account that **X** should contain the features for all instances, while **Y** should contain the class label of all instances.

2. Divide the dataset into training, validation, and testing sets, using a split ratio of 10%:

```
from sklearn.model_selection import train_test_split

X_new, X_test, Y_new, Y_test = train_test_split(X, Y, test_size=0.1,
random_state=101)

X_train, X_dev, Y_train, Y_dev = train_test_split(X_new, Y_new, test_
size=0.12, random_state=101)
```

The final shape of all sets must match the values shown in the following code:

```
X_train = (26048, 9)
Y_train = (26048, )
X_dev = (3256, 9)
Y_dev = (3256, )
X_test = (3257, 9)
Y_test = (3257, )
```

3. Import the Gaussian Naïve Bayes class, and then use the **`fit`** method to train the model over the training sets (**`X_train`** and **`Y_train`**):

```
from sklearn.naive_bayes import GaussianNB

model_NB = GaussianNB()
model_NB.fit(X_train,Y_train)
```

4. Finally, perform a prediction using the model that you trained previously for a new instance with the following values for each feature: 39, 6, 13, 4, 0, 2174, 0, 40, 38.

Using the following code, the prediction for the individual should be equal to zero, which means that the individual most likely has an income below or equal to 50K:

```
pred_1 = model_NB.predict([[39,6,13,4,0,4,1,2174,0,40,38]])
print(pred_1)
```

Activity 12: Training a Decision Tree Model for our Census Income Dataset

The shape of the previously created subsets must be as follows:

```
X_train = (26048, 11)
Y_train = (26048, 1)
X_dev = (3256, 11)
Y_dev = (3256, 1)
X_test = (3257, 11)
Y_test = (3257, 1)
```

1. Using the preprocessed Census Income Dataset that was previously split into the different subsets, import the **DecisionTreeClassifier** class, and then use the **fit** method to train the model over the training sets (**X_train** and **Y_train**):

```
from sklearn.tree import DecisionTreeClassifier

model_tree = DecisionTreeClassifier()
model_tree.fit(X_train,Y_train)
```

2. Finally, perform a prediction using the model that you trained before for a new instance with the following values for each feature: 39, 6, 13, 4, 0, 2174, 0, 40, 38.

   Using the following code, the prediction for the individual should be equal to zero, which means that the individual most likely has an income below or equal to 50K:

```
pred_2 = model_tree.predict([[39,6,13,4,0,4,1,2174,0,40,38]])
print(pred_2)
```

Activity 13: Training a SVM Model for our Census Income Dataset

The shape of the previously created subsets must be as follows:

```
X_train = (26048, 11)
Y_train = (26048, 1)
X_dev = (3256, 11)
Y_dev = (3256, 1)
X_test = (3257, 11)
Y_test = (3257, 1)
```

1. Using the preprocessed Census Income Dataset that was previously split into the different subsets, import the **SVC** class, and then use the **fit** method to train the model over the training sets (**X_train** and **Y_train**):

```
from sklearn.svm import SVC

model_svm = SVC()
model_svm.fit(X_train,Y_train)
```

2. Finally, perform a prediction using the model that you trained before for a new instance with the following values for each feature: 39, 6, 13, 4, 0, 2174, 0, 40, 38.

   Using the following code, the prediction for the individual should be equal to zero, which means that the individual most likely has an income below or equal to 50K:

   ```
   pred_3 = model_svm.predict([[39,6,13,4,0,4,1,2174,0,40,38]])
   print(pred_3)
   ```

Chapter 5: Artificial Neural Networks: Predict Annual Income

Activity 14: Training a Multilayer Perceptron for our Census Income Dataset

1. Using the preprocessed Census Income Dataset, separate the features from the target, creating the variables **X** and **Y**:

```
X = data.drop("target", axis=1)
Y = data["target"]
```

   As explained previously, there are several ways to achieve the separation of **X** and **Y**, and the main thing to consider is that **X** should contain the features for all instances, while **Y** should contain the class label of all instances.

2. Divide the dataset into training, validation, and testing sets, using a split ratio of 10%:

```
from sklearn.model_selection import train_test_split
X_new, X_test, Y_new, Y_test = train_test_split(X, Y, test_size=0.1,
random_state=101)
X_train, X_dev, Y_train, Y_dev = train_test_split(X_new, Y_new, test_
size=0.1111, random_state=101)
```

   The shape of the sets created should be as follows:

```
X_train = (26048, 9)
X_dev = (3256, 9)
X_test = (3257, 9)
Y_train = (26048, )
Y_dev = (3256, )
Y_test = (3257, 1)
```

3. From the **neural_network** module, import the Multilayer Perceptron Classifier class. Initialize it and train the model over the training data.

   Leave the hyperparameters to their default values. Again, use a **random_state** equal to 101:

```
from sklearn.neural_network import MLPClassifier
model = MLPClassifier(random_state=101)
model = model.fit(X_train, Y_train)
```

4. Address any warning that may appear after training the model with the default values for the hyperparameters.

No warning was raised during the training process of the network, which means that the model was able to achieve convergence using the default values for the hyperparameters. Nevertheless, keep in mind that this does not mean that the best model was achieved, and changes in the hyperparameter values may result in better performance of the model.

Calculate the accuracy of the model for all three sets (training, validation, and testing):

```
from sklearn.metrics import accuracy_score

X_sets = [X_train, X_dev, X_test]
Y_sets = [Y_train, Y_dev, Y_test]

accuracy = []

for i in range(0,len(X_sets)):

  pred = model.predict(X_sets[i])
  score = accuracy_score(Y_sets[i], pred)
  accuracy.append(score)
```

The accuracy score for the three sets should be as follows:

```
Train sets = 0.8342
Dev sets = 0.8111
Test sets = 0.8252
```

Activity 15: Comparing Different Models to Choose the Best Fit for the Census Income Data Problem

1. Open the Jupyter Notebook that you used to train the models.
2. Compare the four models based on their accuracy score only.

By taking the accuracy scores of the models from the previous chapter, it is possible to perform a final comparison to choose the model that better solves the data problem. To do so, the following table displays the accuracy scores for all four models:

	Naïve Bayes	Decision Tree	SVM	Multilayer Perceptron
Training sets	0.7970	0.9723	0.9119	0.8508
Validation sets	0.7905	0.8120	0.8015	0.8289
Testing sets	0.8084	0.8228	0.8148	0.8504

Figure 5.17: Accuracy scores of all four models for the Census Income Dataset

To identify the model with the best performance, begin by comparing the accuracy rates over the training sets. From this, it is possible to conclude that the decision tree model is a better fit to the data problem. Nonetheless, the performance over the validation and testing sets is lower than the one achieved using the Multilayer Perceptron, which is an indication of the presence of high variance in the decision tree model.

Hence, a good approach would be to address the high variance of the decision tree model by simplifying the model and adding a pruning argument, for instance (the pruning argument "trims" the leaves of the tree to simplify it and ignore some of the details of the tree in order to generalize the model to the data). Ideally, the model should be able to reach a similar level of accuracy for all three sets, which would make it the best model for the data problem.

However, if the model is not able to overcome this variance, and assuming that all the models have been fine-tuned to achieve the maximum performance possible, the Multilayer Perceptron should be the model that's selected, considering that it performs best over the testing sets. This is mainly because the performance of the model over the testing set is the one that defines its overall performance over unseen data, which means that the one with higher testing set performance will be more useful in the long term.

Chapter 6: Building Your Own Program

Activity 16: Performing the Preparation and Creation Stages for the Bank Marketing Dataset

For the purpose of this demonstration, a **random_state** equal to 100 will be used for the following solution:

1. Open a Jupyter Notebook to implement this activity and import **pandas**:

```
import pandas as pd
```

2. Load the previously downloaded dataset into the notebook:

```
data = pd.read_csv("../datasets/bank-full.csv")
```

The first 10 rows of the dataset can be seen using the statement **data.head(10)**:

	age	job	marital	education	default	balance	housing	loan	contact	day	month	duration	campaign	pdays	previous	poutcome	y
0	58	management	married	tertiary	no	2143	yes	no	NaN	5	may	261	1	-1	0	NaN	no
1	44	technician	single	secondary	no	29	yes	no	NaN	5	may	151	1	-1	0	NaN	no
2	33	entrepreneur	married	secondary	no	2	yes	yes	NaN	5	may	76	1	-1	0	NaN	no
3	47	blue-collar	married	NaN	no	1506	yes	no	NaN	5	may	92	1	-1	0	NaN	no
4	33	NaN	single	NaN	no	1	no	no	NaN	5	may	198	1	-1	0	NaN	no
5	35	management	married	tertiary	no	231	yes	no	NaN	5	may	139	1	-1	0	NaN	no
6	28	management	single	tertiary	no	447	yes	yes	NaN	5	may	217	1	-1	0	NaN	no
7	42	entrepreneur	divorced	tertiary	yes	2	yes	no	NaN	5	may	380	1	-1	0	NaN	no
8	58	retired	married	primary	no	121	yes	no	NaN	5	may	50	1	-1	0	NaN	no
9	43	technician	single	secondary	no	593	yes	no	NaN	5	may	55	1	-1	0	NaN	no

Figure 6.6: A screenshot showing the first 10 instances of the dataset

The missing values are shown as **NaN**, as explained previously.

3. Select the metric that's the most appropriate for measuring the performance of the model, considering that the purpose of the study is to detect clients who would subscribe to the term deposit.

The metric to evaluate the performance of the model is the precision metric, as it compares the correctly classified positive labels against the total number of instances predicted as positive.

4. Preprocess the dataset.

Handling Missing Values

Use the following code to check for missing values:

```
data.isnull().sum()
```

Based on the results, you will observe that only four features contain missing values: **job** (288), **education** (1,857), **contact** (13,020), and **poutcome** (36,959).

The first two features can be left unhandled considering that the missing values represent less than the 5% of the entire data. On the other hand, 28.8% of the values are missing from the **contact** feature, and taking into account that the feature refers to the mode of contact, which is irrelevant for determining whether a person will subscribe to a new product, it is safe to remove this feature from the study. Finally, the **poutcome** feature is missing 81.7% of its values, which is why this feature is also removed from the study.

Using the following code, the preceding two features are dropped:

```
data = data.drop(["contact", "poutcome"], axis=1)
```

Converting the Categorical Features into Numeric Form

For all nominal features, use the following code:

```
from sklearn.preprocessing import LabelEncoder
enc = LabelEncoder()

features_to_convert = ["job", "marital", "default", "housing", "loan",
"month", "y"]

for i in features_to_convert:
  data[i] = enc.fit_transform(data[i].astype("str"))
```

The preceding code, as explained in previous chapters, converts all the qualitative features into their numeric forms.

Next, to handle the ordinal feature, we must use the following code:

```
data["education"] = data["education"].fillna["unknown"]
encoder = ["unknown", "primary", "secondary", "tertiary"]

for i, word in enumerate(encoder):
  data["education"] = data["education"].str.replace(word,str(i))
  data["education"] = data["education"].astype("int64")
```

Here, the first line converts **NaN** values to the word **unknown** and the second line sets the order of the values in the feature. Next, a **for** loop is used to replace each word for a number that follows an order. For the preceding example, 0 will be used to replace the word **unknown**, then 1 will be used instead of **primary**, and so on. Finally, the whole column is converted into an integer type since the **replace** function writes down the numbers as strings.

Dealing with Outliers

Use the following code to check for outliers:

```
outliers = []

for i in range(data.shape[1]):
  min_t = data[data.columns[i]].mean() - (3 * data[data.columns[i]].std())
  max_t = data[data.columns[i]].mean() + (3 * data[data.columns[i]].std())
  count = 0

  for j in data[data.columns[i]]:
    if j < min_t or j > max_t:
      count += 1

  outliers[data.columns[i]] = [count, data.shape[0]-count]
```

By analyzing the results from the preceding code, you will observe that the outliers do not account for more than 5% of the total values in each feature, which is why they can be left unhandled.

5. Separate the features from the class label and split the dataset into three sets (training, validation, and testing).

   To separate the features from the target value, use the following code:

   ```
   X = data.drop("y", axis = 1)
   Y = data["y"]
   ```

   Next, to perform a split of the form 60/20/20%, use the following code:

   ```
   from sklearn.model_selection import train_test_split
   X_new, X_test, Y_new, Y_test = train_test_split(X, Y, test_size = 0.2,
   random_state = 0)
   X_train, X_dev, Y_train, Y_dev = train_test_split(X_new, Y_new, test_size
   = 0.25, random_state = 0)
   ```

The shape of each set is as follows:

```
X_train = (27126, 14)
Y_train = (27126, )
X_dev = (9042, 14)
Y_dev = (9042, )
X_test = (9043, 14)
Y_test = (9043, )
```

6. Use the Decision Tree and the Multilayer Perceptron algorithms to apply over the dataset and train the models.

   By using the following code, both algorithms can be trained:

```
from sklearn.tree import DecisionTreeClassifier
model_tree = DecisionTreeClassifier(random_state = 101)
model_tree.fit(X_train, Y_train)

from sklearn.neural_network import MLPClassifier
model_NN = MLPClassifier(random_state = 101)
model_NN.fit(X_train, Y_train)
```

7. Evaluate both models by using the metric that was selected previously.

   Using the following code, it is possible to measure the precision score of the Decision Tree model:

```
from sklearn.metrics import precision_score
X_sets = [X_train, X_dev, X_test]
Y_sets = [Y_train, Y_dev, Y_test]

precision = []

for i in range(0, len(X_sets)):
  pred = model_tree.predict(X_sets[i])
  score = precision_score(Y_sets[i], pred)
  precision.append(score)
```

   The same code can be modified to calculate the score for the Multilayer Perceptron.

The results from the code are shown in the following table:

	Decision Tree	Multilayer Perceptron
Training sets	1.00	0.60
Validation sets	0.43	0.56
Testing sets	0.43	0.53

Figure 6.7: Precision scores for both models

8. Fine-tune some of the hyperparameters to fix the issues detected during the evaluation of the model by performing error analysis.

   Although the precision of the decision tree over the training sets is perfect, on comparing it against the results of the other two sets, it is possible to conclude that the model suffers from high variance.

   On the other hand, the Multilayer Perceptron has a similar performance on all three sets, but the overall performance is low, which means that the model is more likely to be suffering from high bias.

   Considering this, for the decision tree model, both the minimum number of samples required to be at a leaf node and the maximum depth of the tree are changed in order to simplify the model. On the other hand, for the Multilayer Perceptron, the number of iterations, the number of hidden layers, the number of units in each layer, and the tolerance for optimization are changed.

   The following code shows the final values used for each hyperparameter, considering that to arrive at them it is required to try different values:

```
from sklearn.tree import DecisionTreeClassifier
model_tree = DecisionTreeClassifier(randome_state = 101, min_samples_leaf =
100, max_depth = 100)
model_tree.fit(X_train, Y_train)

from sklearn.neural_network import MLPClassifier
model_NN = MLPClassifier(random_state = 101, max_iter = 1000, hidden_layer_
sizes = [100,100,50,25,25], tol=1e-7)
model_NN.fit(X_train, Y_train)
```

9. Compare the final versions of your models and select the one that you consider best fits the data.

   By calculating the precision score for all three sets for the newly trained models, we obtain the following values:

	Decision Tree	Multilayer Perceptron
Training sets	0.61	0.64
Validation sets	0.57	0.60
Testing sets	0.54	0.59

Figure 6.8: Precision scores for the newly trained models

An improvement in performance for both models is achieved, and by comparing the values, it is possible to conclude that the Multilayer Perceptron outperforms the Decision Tree. Based on this, the Multilayer Perceptron is selected as the better model to solve the data problem.

Activity 17: Saving and Loading the Final Model for the Bank Marketing Dataset

1. Save the model into a file named `final_model.pkl`:

```
path = os.getcwd() + "/final_model.pkl"
file = open(path, "wb")
pickle.dump(model_NN, file)
```

2. Open a new Jupyter Notebook and import the required modules and class:

```
from sklearn.neural_network import MLPClassifier
import pickle
import os
```

3. Load the model:

```
path = os.getcwd() + "/final_model.pkl"
file = open(path, "rb")
model = pickle.load(file)
```

4. Perform a prediction for an individual by using the following values:

   42, 2, 0, 0, 1, 2, 1, 0, 5, 8, 380, 1, -1, 0.

   ```
   pred = model.predict([[42,2,0,0,1,2,1,0,5,8,380,1,-1,0]])
   ```

   By printing the **pred** variable, the output is **0**, which is the numeric form of **No**. This means that the individual is more likely to not subscribe to the new product.

Activity 18: Allowing Interaction with the Bank Marketing Dataset Model

1. In a text editor, create a class object that contains two main functions. One should be an initializer that loads the model, and the other should be a **predict** method where the data is fed to the model to retrieve an output:

   ```
   import pandas as pd
   import pickle
   import os
   from sklearn.neural_network import MLPClassifier

   Class NN_Model(object):

     def __init__(self):
       path = os.getcwd() + "/model_exercise.pkl"
       file = open(path, "rb")
       self.model = pickle.load(file)

     def predict(self, age, job, marital, education, default, balance,
   housing, loan, day, month, duration, campaign, pdays, previous):
       X = [[age, job, marital, education, default, balance, housing, loan,
   day, month, duration, campaign, pdays, previous]]
       return self.model.predict(X)
   ```

2. In a Jupyter Notebook, import and initialize the class that you created in the last step. Next, create the variables that will hold the values for the features and use the following values: 42, 2, 0, 0, 1, 2, 1, 0, 5, 8, 380, 1, -1, 0.

```
from trainedModel import NN_Model

model = NN_Model()

age = 42
job = 2
marital = 0
education = 0
default = 1
balance = 2
housing = 1
loan = 0
day = 5
month = 8
duration = 380
campaign = 1
pdays = -1
previous = 0
```

3. Perform a prediction by applying the **predict** method:

```
pred = model.predict(age=age, job=job, marital=marital,
education=education, default=default, balance=balance, housing=housing,
loan=loan, day=day, month=month, duration=duration, campaign=campaign,
pdays=pdays, previous=previous)
```

By printing the variable, the prediction is equal to **0**; that is, the individual with the given features is not likely to subscribe to the product.

Index

About

All major keywords used in this book are captured alphabetically in this section. Each one is accompanied by the page number of where they appear.

A

B

C

D

E

F

G

H

I

J

K

L

M

N

O

P

R

S

T

U

V

W

www.ingramcontent.com/pod-product-compliance
Lightning Source LLC
Chambersburg PA
CBHW080638060326
40690CB00021B/4988
* 9 7 8 1 7 8 9 8 0 3 5 5 6 *